WHEN LOVE BITES

WHEN LOVE BITES

written by **CATHY PRESS**

illustrated by DAVE SHEPHARD
designed by SMART DESIGN STUDIO

Contents

Foreword   07

Introduction   10

PART 1: RECOGNISE CONTROLLING BEHAVIOURS

Chapter 1: **Control in Relationships**   17

Chapter 2: **The Partner**   35

Chapter 3: **The Controller**   47

Chapter 4: **The Charmer**   55

Chapter 5: **The Bully**   79

Chapter 6: **The Mindmixer**   101

Chapter 7: **The Taker**   137

Chapter 8: **The Keeper**   179

Chapter 9: **How to Spot the Controller**   203

PART 2: TAKE BACK CONTROL

Chapter 10: **Dealing with Feelings of Overwhelm**   215

Chapter 11: **Developing Your Self-Esteem and Confidence**   231

Chapter 12: **Staying Safe Online**   241

Chapter 13: **What if I Want to Leave?**   249

Conclusion   270

Glossary   274

Places to Get Help   277

Afterword   284

About the Author   288

LIST OF BOXES

Hormones	36
Passive aggressive behaviour	63
The cycle of abuse	68
Toxic masculinity	86
Anger	94
Gaslighting	110
Saying 'No'	142
Rape and sexual assault	144
Pornography	147
Revenge porn	149
Consent	154
The difference between feeling ashamed and shame	164
Self-harm	165
Five Fs – friend, fight, flight, freeze and flop	168
Know yourself	204
Self-regulation	221
My personal rights	273
Escape the Trap	286

Foreword

By Rachel Williams and Celia Peachey

Rachel Williams

As a survivor of domestic violence and abuse myself, I was excited to read *When Love Bites*. Having been in a toxic, unhealthy relationship aged 21, with no real experience of what a healthy relationship should look like, I was aware that this book had a lot to cover – especially knowing now what I sadly didn't know then. Had I possessed all this knowledge and understanding it would have saved me 18 years of being abused and the tragic loss of my 16-year-old son, Jack.

If you are unfortunate enough to find yourself in an abusive relationship, it can destroy your mind and soul. You really do lose your identity and worth as a person. This book will help you understand the ugly facets of domestic abuse. It will help not just victims and survivors of domestic abuse, but also teachers, parents, carers and – most importantly – you, the next generation. Understanding how domestic abuse presents is the only that way we will break the cycle of abuse. Education is key to tackling this abhorrent crime.

Having read *When Love Bites*, I feel truly humbled to write this foreword. Anyone who reads this book will gain a greater level of understanding of what holds a person in an abusive relationship and why victims sometimes can't just leave. Readers will also be able to spot the behaviours of an abusive partner and will see the difference between a healthy and unhealthy relationship.

I urge you to read this book, share your knowledge and understanding with others, and to never feel ashamed if you have been abused. The shame should always lie at the feet of those who consciously choose to abuse.

Rachel Williams is Founder of Stand Up to Domestic Abuse (SUTDA).

Celia Peachey

Now more than ever young people can empower themselves with awareness and the tools for psychological, emotional and social change by identifying patterns of behaviours and where they come from.

My childhood was very troubled, my family fragmented and dysfunctional because domestic abuse was normalised. I had no idea what was happening, I just knew I was suffering and needed to radically change my life.

In my twenties I went on a journey of self-discovery – I needed to because I felt all areas of my life were a mess. The catalyst for my profoundest transformation was in discovering that my mum had been murdered and how even the police didn't see the warning signs. This happens far too often and the damage and loss are irreparable.

I've had to dig deep in my soul, learning to ask better questions to gain better answers and solutions. I sought out books, teachers and healers to expand my awareness for self-understanding, and to craft my character to co-create better relationships. In effect, I rebuilt my life myself.

With 40 per cent of teenagers currently in unhealthy relationships, it's clear that education is the key to 'escaping the trap'. Education creates awareness, which in turn creates choices.

I know first-hand how the right tools can bring about dramatic change.

I love Cathy's book: it's a clear and vibrant exploration of the many healthy and unhealthy dynamics in relationships. *When Love Bites* is packed with practical wisdom to help anyone identify the dynamics or power imbalances in their relationship. Identifying the many guises and behaviours of your partner, and where these beliefs come from, enables you to distinguish whether your relationship is unhealthy.

Don't just read this book; work your way through it, make notes, do the exercises, and ask questions and have the conversations needed to cultivate clarity and empowerment in your relationships.

When Love Bites offers insights that support the simple truth I live by – that 'prevention is the cure'. Its contribution to the next generation is that **you don't have to endure the heartache of unconscious toxic relationships**. *When Love Bites* shows that **you have a choice**. The book offers guidance and affirms that you can choose wisely and cultivate wholesome and life-affirming relationships with healthy boundaries for a brilliant and bright future.

Celia Peachey is Founder and CEO of Ultimate Alchemist.

INTRODUCTION

Firstly, a massive thank you for picking up *When Love Bites* and giving it a go! **This book is for every young person who has found themselves with a partner who thinks it is acceptable to use abusive behaviour towards you.** It doesn't matter whether you identify as heterosexual or LGBTQ+, this book is inclusive and is for you.

It is estimated that at least 40 per cent of all young people experience abuse within their early relationships, and it makes no difference how long those relationships last or the gender of the partners. Further, it is likely that those same people will experience abusive behaviours in future relationships, all of which will affect their wellbeing – physically, socially and sexually, and/or impact their emotional and mental health. This book aims to make clear that **you are not responsible for the way you are treated by your partner or for how you feel about yourself as a result of their behaviour**. You can only be responsible for your own behaviour, and in turn, your partner is responsible for the way they choose to behave towards you. If you believe that your relationship – past or present – was or is bad and 'it's all your fault' or 'you were/are the problem' or 'you were/are responsible for meeting your partner's needs', then read on. This book explores what happens to us in relationships that are less than comfortable and happy. It gives an in-depth explanation of the many different types of abusive behaviour, who is actually responsible for this behaviour and, more importantly, how this behaviour may have impacted you and the way you see yourself. Having awareness is the first step to protecting yourself.

The book is structured in two parts. Part 1 focuses on identifying the many controlling and coercive behaviours of an abusive partner – referred to in this book as the 'Controller' – and how we are affected by such abusive behaviour. Part 2 provides ideas on what you can do if you find yourself on the receiving end of an abusive partner. Each chapter has a specific focus so you can either read *When Love Bites* from cover to cover or dip into whichever chapter seems most relevant to you in the moment. That said, no matter what order you read the chapters in, aim to read the whole book because you will start to identify your partner's behaviour and aspects about yourself – your experiences, thoughts and feelings.

I was inspired to write *When Love Bites* as a result of working over three decades as a psychotherapist with thousands of people, both teenagers and adults and encompassing all sexual orientations, who have had long histories of relationship abuse. Much of this suffering could have been avoided if they had had access to the knowledge, insight and learning in their teenage years to support them to recognise abusive behaviours and the direct impact of this behaviour on their wellbeing and sense of self. Many young people today experience some of the most severe forms of abusive behaviour by their partners while they still live at home with their parents; it doesn't only take place behind closed doors after they have started to live with their partner.

The term 'Controller' together with the defining characters of the Charmer, the Bully, the Mindmixer, the Taker and the Keeper, were developed alongside young people in the early months of creating the Escape the Trap programme (see page 286).

Relationships are **complex** and often **tricky to navigate**, even for the most experienced and switched-on person. Many of us have rushed to pair up with a partner in that first flush of love to have a 'grown-up' relationship. This is quite normal and is part of how we develop and learn. However, as you read through *When Love Bites*, I hope you will take a step back and consider what kind of partner you would like to be in a relationship with. You deserve to be in a relationship with someone of your choice, not necessarily the first person who shows an interest in you. Further, I hope you will reflect on what kind of partner you want to be. Do you need saving by your 'Prince Charming' or celebrated and cherished by your partner as an equal? You know that there is no such thing as Disney love!

Finally, you may recognise that you use some of the behaviours described in this book. This is normal. It might be an uncomfortable experience, but it is worth being honest with yourself and acknowledging your own behaviours. Noticing our own behaviour is the first step to changing it. For instance, if you feel insecure and worried about 'losing' your relationship you may unconsciously support this with your own unhelpful, distorted beliefs and attitudes, thus giving yourself permission to 'hurt the one you love'. Rather than continuing in the same way, be reassured that you can change this thinking if you want to, a bit like reprogramming a computer. The key is to take responsibility for your own behaviour and be genuinely motivated to behave differently. **Your partner isn't responsible for making you feel good about yourself – you are.** By becoming aware of how you behave and making changes, you will move towards more fulfilling and loving relationships in the future. There is hope!

Part 1:

RECOGNISE

CONTR

BEHAV

Recognise Controlling Behaviours

Part 1 looks at control in relationships and introduces the different characters of the Controller, who uses controlling and coercive behaviours to abuse others. It also describes the qualities of the Partner, who represents the caring, respectful and loving person that we all deserve to be in a relationship with. Being in an abusive relationship can have a real impact on how you see yourself, but hopefully once you can identify the Controller's behaviours and where their beliefs come from, you will be able to understand that how you feel is directly related to how you are treated. Information on how to get help is included, which may be helpful as you reflect on your experiences.

Chapter 1
CONTROL IN RELATIONSHIPS

When we first get involved in a relationship, we never imagine that it will turn sour. We tend to view a new relationship warmly and with hope that it will bring good experiences. It can therefore be very confusing to understand what is going on when the relationship doesn't pan out in this way; for example, if your partner is changing their behaviour and mood from one minute to the next, appearing to be both nice and nasty to you. This type of behaviour is typical of a controlling and abusive relationship. This chapter explores the controlling relationship and will explain controlling behaviour and coercive behaviour.

What is control?

The most important thing to consider when looking at your own relationships is the context. Looking at the circumstances around your relationship gives you a better picture of what it is really like. A one-off behaviour is defined as such because it only happens once; for example, being shouted at, being ignored, being criticised or being compared to someone else. In a relationship with a loving partner you would be safe to tell them that you didn't like how you were treated; your loving partner would apologise, take responsibility for their behaviour and wouldn't do it again! However, when you start to experience a few of these behaviours working together it creates a different context where we identify patterns of coercive and controlling behaviour. Every person in an abusive relationship experiences some or all of these behaviours, no matter what their age. You will discover in much more depth what controlling behaviours are and how to recognise them in **Chapters 2** to **9**.

18

The following is the legal definition of **Domestic Violence (2013)**:[1]

Any incident or pattern of incidents of controlling, coercive or threatening behaviour, violence or abuse between those aged **16 or over** who are or have been intimate partners or family members regardless of gender or sexuality. This can encompass, but is not limited to, the following types of abuse: psychological, physical, sexual, financial and emotional.

Controlling behaviour is: a range of acts designed to make a person subordinate and/or dependent by isolating them from sources of support, exploiting their resources and capacities for personal gain, depriving them of the means needed for independence, resistance and escape and regulating their everyday behaviour.

Coercive behaviour is: an act or a pattern of acts of assault, threats, humiliation and intimidation or other abuse that is used to harm, punish, or frighten their victim.

This includes issues of concern to black and minority ethnic (BAME) communities such as so-called 'honour-based violence', female genital mutilation (FGM) and forced marriage, and it is clear that victims are not confined to one gender or ethnic group.

This definition may seem hard to take in at first, so let's break it down.

---

[1] This definition is correct at the time of writing but may change as the new Domestic Abuse Bill comes into force.

Controlling Behaviour

No matter what the starting point is in your relationship, a controlling and abusive partner will find ways to literally shrink your world and your life as you know it. They will squeeze out the other people in your life – your friends and family – and the things you love to do such as your studies, hobbies, interests and activities. They might take your money or possessions and give you rules about what you can and can't do. When your world becomes so much smaller in this way, you can easily become more dependent on your partner.

'A range of acts designed to make a person subordinate' means:

- **Doing things to make you feel inferior, such as comparing how you look to others or telling you they would fancy you more if you changed how you look.**

- **Doing things to make you feel insignificant, such as ignoring you or speaking over you or telling you people don't like you.**

- **Doing things to make you feel of no value, such as making fun of your opinions and ideas or excluding you by not inviting you to go out with them and their friends.**

- **Doing things to make you feel less than equal, lower than or less than you should about yourself, such as saying you aren't clever enough to do what you dream of or constantly putting you down.**

'Dependent by isolating them from sources of support' means stopping you having access to people who could support you such as your family, friends or professionals – in person or online.

'Exploiting their resources and capacities for personal gain' means they might prevent you from pursuing your education, taking up the opportunity to have a job and keep it, achieving your goals and, ultimately, to have new experiences.

'Depriving them of the means needed for independence, resistance and escape' means they might take and control your money and/or your possessions (e.g. your phone or travel card), which prevents you from getting to school, college or work, and stops you from earning money or doing anything that would increase your opportunity to be independent. If you don't have access to your own money, it is harder to leave the relationship. If you are physically injured and overwhelmed, you may feel too exhausted to resist and find a way to make yourself safe.

'Regulating their everyday behaviour' means demanding to know about everything you do, making you justify where you have been, who you have been with and why. It includes putting restrictions on you about who you can and can't talk to, where you can and can't go, telling you how long you should be, imposing a list of rules about what you should and shouldn't be doing, and using any means needed to ensure you always obey and comply with their rules.

Coercive Behaviour

You know you are being coerced when you find yourself doing something because you think you **have** to, not because you **want** to. For example, you will be worried and/or scared about your partner's reaction and what will happen if you don't do what they want. As a result, you are trapped within your shrunken world with no freedom of choice.

'An act or a pattern of acts of assault, threats, humiliation and intimidation or other abuse that is used to harm, punish, or frighten their victim' means behaviours and tactics which directly threaten you, like the use of physical abuse and violence, of embarrassing you and making you feel stupid, small and worthless, either when you are alone with them or more publicly, in front of others, perhaps even online, as well as bullying or terrorising you by their behaviour. All of this is intended to hurt you, to punish you and to make you feel so scared of what they might do to you that you can't stand up for yourself or consider leaving them. You feel **trapped**.

Coercive control is a criminal offence and applies both in the context of an intimate relationship (you and your partner) and family relationships (sibling to sibling, child to parent, etc.). It centres around patterns of controlling or coercive behaviours as already discussed and can result in a fine and/or up to five years' imprisonment, which shows how serious it is!

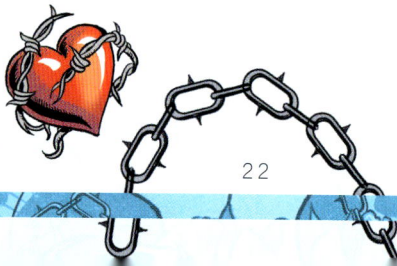

Coercive control is identified by the following points. To illustrate the context let's imagine that you're in a relationship with Sam.

Sam uses controlling or coercive behaviour 'repeatedly or continuously' towards you, i.e. on an ongoing basis.

Sam's pattern of behaviour has a 'serious effect' on you: you either fear violence will be used against you (it only has to be on 'at least two occasions') or it has caused you serious alarm or distress which has had a significant impact on your day-to-day activities.

Sam's behaviour must be such that Sam knows, or ought to know, that it will have a serious effect on you.

Sam (the abuser) and you (the abused) have to be personally connected when the incidents took place; for example, you were and/or have been in an intimate relationship.

You can see that context is extremely important: it provides you with a full picture of what is happening to you, the intention of the Controller (see **Chapter 3**) and the far-reaching impact on you of their controlling and coercive behaviour.

Interestingly, there isn't a definition specifically to describe teenage relationship abuse. In my workshops on relationship abuse and the Escape the Trap programme, young people have come up with their own definitions of coercive and controlling behaviour, for example:

when you are **emotionally mugged off!**

When you are in a relationship that involves being hurt on your body by any unwanted physical contact or hitting, control over your movements and who your friends are, not having the freedom you need, making you do something you do not want to do - for example, <u>ANY</u> unwanted sexual behaviours.

When your boyfriend/girlfriend/partner makes you <u>feel bad</u> or <u>hurts</u> <u>you</u>.

When love don't make you feel bad!

When your partner makes you or convinces you to do things that you don't want to do by making you feel bad, NOT good enough, frightened, frigid or boring if you say 'no'. This puts them in a position of control over you.

When someone is saying, doing or threatening something that makes you say, do or feel things that you don't want to.

What Type of Person Behaves Abusively to Others?

Many people think that individuals who behave abusively towards others do so because they have been treated poorly themselves, conditioned by their family to believe it is the normal way to behave, or that they might have very low self-esteem and somehow it enables them to feel powerful.

I, too, held this belief about why my abusive partners were abusive towards me. I spent years trying to see the world through their eyes in order to understand how their behaviour towards me was the result of how they had been treated themselves. Finally, I understood that their behaviour was not due to their experiences. Many people who have been treated very badly in their early years and have suffered in various ways wouldn't dream of hurting someone else or using that as an excuse.

The graphic on pages 26 and 27 illustrates ideas supplied by young people of what kind of person behaves abusively in a relationship. Many of these suggest that there must be something wrong with the person; for example, they have poor mental health, a poor family background or are someone who acts tough all the time. A person may be fearful of someone – a family member, someone in their peer group, school or college or the people in their neighbourhood – and as a consequence can behave defensively to mask their fear. But this doesn't automatically make that person hurt the one they are in a relationship with. The truth is that anyone –

whether their life experience has been good or bad – can behave in this way, simply because they believe they have the right to do so. You may identify that many of the reasons included in the graphic are actually excuses for the abusive behaviour.

WHAT KIND OF PERSON BEHAVES ABUSIVELY IN A RELATIONSHIP?

BAD BOY/BITCH

Criminal

INSECURE

PERVERT

POOR

VULNERABLE

HAS ADHD

ANYONE

HAS ADD

THINKS IT'S FUNNY

DRUG ADDICT

OLDER

Psycho

HAS NO MORALS

DESPERATE

ROUGH AND READY

LONER

CONTROLLING ALCOHOLIC

NO STATUS

GANG MEMBER

AUTISTIC

HAS abusive PARENTS

NARCISSIST

SPOILT IDIOT CHAV LOSER

DICK HEAD PAEDOPHILE

BiG STRONG NEEDY G NUTTER MANIPULATIVE

GREW UP IN A ROUGH AREA

BULLY VICTIM OF ABUSE HAS MENTAL HEALTH ISSUES JEALOUS

BELIEVE THEY HAVE THE RIGHT WIMP DOMINATING WEIRDO

Angry

UNLOVED BY FAMILY

WHAT TYPE OF PERSON MIGHT BE VICTIM TO TEENAGE RELATIONSHIP ABUSE?

Many teenagers experience relationships that are abusive, coercive and controlling. Studies estimate that about 40 per cent of young people are in abusive relationships at any given time. However, this is probably an underestimate: there are thousands of young people experiencing abusive relationships who don't tell anyone what is happening to them and are therefore not included in any of the studies undertaken. From my experience of working with teenagers in a professional capacity, I would estimate that at least half, if not two thirds, of all young people experience some form of relationship abuse at least once.

As you read this book, you may recognise that you are in, or have been in, this situation yourself. You may not have looked at your relationship in this way before and very likely you would not have identified yourself as a victim. Maybe you thought what was happening to you was 'normal'.

Victims of relationship abuse are found in every type of community, as are those who use abusive behaviour. Sadly, the society, culture and faith systems in which you live can hold very strong judgements about the kind of person who finds themselves a victim of relationship abuse. Some of these judgements are harsh and unkind and strongly imply that the person who is a victim has something wrong with them. But the victim isn't the one being cruel and unkind. The following graphic illustrates some ideas that have come from young people I have worked with.

WHAT TYPE OF PERSON IS THE VICTIM OF ABUSE?

ATTENTION-SEEKER

ANY CULTURE   UNCONFIDENT   CHILDISH

UNPOPULAR   NEGLECTED

TOO SEXUAL   HOMELESS   SHY   MOUTHY

YOUNG MUM   GIRLS

DOESN'T TAKE CARE OF THEMSELVES

SLAG   **BULLIED**   LADETTE   UNLOVED

HAS A LEARNING DISABILITY   TROUBLEMAKER

IS IN A SAME-SEX RELATIONSHIP

FAT   POOR   VULNERABLE   NAÏVE

DOESN'T HAVE FRIENDS OR FAMILY

NO PRIDE   PUSHOVER   QUIET   DESPERATE

ANY GENDER   LONER   IN SOCIAL CARE

HAS ALREADY BEEN A VICTIM

Has an abusive father   JEALOUS

IDIOT   FRIGID   **HAS NO MORALS**

HAS A BAD HOME LIFE   **UGLY**   ANYONE

PREGNANT

SELF-CENTRED   YOUNGER   WEAK   HAS LOW SELF-ESTEEM

DESERVES IT   INEXPERIENCED   GEEK

ASKS FOR IT   THINKS IT IS NORMAL   HAS MENTAL HEALTH ISSUES

Slut   STUPID   CHEAP

Risk Factors

Absolutely **anyone** can be vulnerable to relationship abuse and exploitation from their so-called 'partner'. Situations that can increase the risk faced by young people include:

- Previous experience of violence in the home
- Depression in childhood
- Poor mental health
- Drug and alcohol misuse from an early age
- School non-attendance
- Early sexual relationships
- Involvement with gangs
- Experience of child sexual exploitation
- Sexual and/or gender identity can create risk if you are not yet 'out' to family and friends
- Being in a peer group that sees coercive behaviour as 'normal'
- Having a child as a teenager
- It is the first relationship
- Disruption of family unit
- Being a 'looked-after child'
- Poor or non-communicative relationship with parents
- Low resilience
- Prone to taking risks
- HBV/forced marriage
- Has physical disability
- Has learning disability
- If the abusing partner is two or more years older than the victim.

A person may not have experienced any of the 'risk factors' or identify with the judgements made about what kind of person becomes a victim, and yet they may still find themselves in an early abusive relationship. If it can happen to you, it can clearly happen to anyone in any part of your community. And if you understand that being involved in a coercive, controlling and/or dangerous relationship can happen to anyone, it may help you to be less judgemental and have more compassion towards yourself as well as those others who, like you, find themselves in that situation.

What expectations do you have of your relationships?

You may have strong ideas of what your relationships should be like and how they might make you feel, and **Chapter 2** explores ideas about the ideal partner. Your first relationships are intensely felt and are very important to you when you are in them. This is partly because you haven't got lots of relationship experience to compare them with. When it comes to love and relationships, most people are idealists and can believe at the start of each new relationship that it might be the 'real deal'.

Your expectations of what a relationship should be like are heavily influenced by society, culture and the media – music, music videos and films, games and imagery in adverts and social media (Facebook, Instagram, etc.) – in terms of how you 'should' experience yourself and your partner. For example, a partner's excessive jealousy, possessiveness and obsessive demands are often viewed with the romanticised idea that this behaviour is 'proof of their passion', and teenage abusers often justify the use of violence and controlling behaviours as acts of love. **No matter what you are led to believe about relationships, your expectations, and how it 'should' feel to be with someone, the chances are that this is not at all how you experience them.** The reality of many aspects of life is often very different from what popular culture will have us believe.

THINGS YOU MIGHT EXPECT FROM YOUR RELATIONSHIP

ROMANTIC GREAT SEX CUDDLES EXCITING IDEAL THE 'REAL' THING PROTECTED AFFECTIONATE RESPECT FAITHFUL HONEST FUN PERFECT SOULMATES MONEY HUGS FACEBOOK GROWN UP LIFE-CHANGING INSTA OFFICIAL OFFICIAL DON'T NEED ANYONE ELSE SECURITY STATUS FAIRY-TALE ROMANCE TOGETHER FOREVER FAMILY LOOKED AFTER TRUSTING MORE RESPECT WITH PEERS MARRIAGE SEE EACH OTHER CAR TO TAKE ME OUT EVERY DAY GIFTS BABIES SAFE PROTECTIVE KISSES x

Is my partner abusive?

If you answer '**yes**' to any of the questions below, it's possible that you are in an abusive relationship and you should definitely keep reading this book. Of course, some of these behaviours could be put down to immaturity – your partner might have been spoilt by their parents, or perhaps feels entitled or is arrogant, or their lack of experience in relationships may be the reason. However, it is important to remember that **all behaviours form a context** and you should not ignore them.

	YES	NO
Does your partner find it difficult to compromise if they don't get their own way?		
Does your partner pressurise you to respond quickly to text messages, emails or phone calls?		
Does your partner act in a possessive or jealous way with you?		
Does your partner ever call you names, threaten you, or try to make you feel bad?		
Does your partner ever demand that you look a particular way in terms of clothing, hair or make-up?		
Does your partner ever hurt you physically?		
Does your partner try to keep you from seeing your friends or family?		
When with your partner, do you find it difficult to say 'no' to things you don't want to do (e.g. sex)?		
Does your partner like to tell you what to do?		
Has your partner's behaviour towards you changed or got worse recently?		

THE PARTNER

Chapter 2
THE PARTNER

We all have our own idea of what our ideal Partner is like. This chapter explores what it might be like to be with someone who is truly into you and thinks you're awesome, rather than someone who tries to control your every move, i.e. the Controller (see **Chapter 3**).

Falling in love is an intense, wonderful experience. It can make you feel nervous, **dizzy**, **nauseous**, **SWEATY**, **TINGLY** and as if you have *butterflies* in your belly. There is no set formula for falling in love and often no clear reason — it's just chemistry! However, one thing is for sure: it can take you by surprise and feel overwhelming. Almost everyone experiences the feeling of falling in love at least once in their lifetime. Sadly, sometimes people fall in love with people who aren't quite right for them — or right for anyone, for that matter! Being with someone who is rude and/or arrogant, or they physically hurt you, can have a huge impact on how you feel about yourself.

HORMONES

In the context of intimate relationships, hormones have a big part to play.

LUST is powered by testosterone and oestrogen: these hormones drive the desire for sexual pleasure and gratification. They are often identified as being 'male' and 'female', but in reality everyone has a level of testosterone and oestrogen impacting their libido.

ATTRACTION is powered by dopamine (associated with reward and addiction), norepinephrine (associated with stress hormones) and serotonin (associated with stabilising our mood and it gives us a sense of wellbeing). When we are attracted to another person higher levels of dopamine and norepinephrine are released, making us feel giddy, energised and euphoric, and producing the experience of butterflies in our tummy and a smaller appetite; and for some, they can cause insomnia. It is like the feeling of being so 'in love' that you can't eat or sleep, and is a similar response to that of feeling stressed and in high alert. When we are highly attracted to another person it is thought that the increase in testosterone can also suppress serotonin, affecting our mood and decreasing our appetite.

ATTACHMENT is driven by oxytocin and vasopressin. Oxytocin is typically released after sex or strong intimate contact. It is the hormone that forges our experience of bonding and strong connection. On the flip side, if the relationship is on a downturn, things will feel very different when the relationship becomes erratic and unsafe and the connection you had with your partner seems to be lost. When we lose a relationship, we experience some withdrawal of dopamine and oxytocin and it can feel like we crave the person we can no longer see or be in a relationship with. This is when love hurts.

WHAT DOES THE IDEAL PARTNER LOOK LIKE?

Sometimes it can feel like you're never going to meet someone special. However, there is definitely someone out there who you will really connect with. In this book, that person is referred to as the **Partner**: they are like a 'best' friend, they're easy to fall in love with and, better still, you fancy them.

The Partner genuinely likes you; they are truly interested in you and how you are feeling. They listen to you and validate your emotions. The Partner feels comfortable in themselves.

Whereas the Controller might say 'Stop crying, you're over-reacting', the Partner will say words to the effect, 'That must have been really hard for you, I'm so sorry that happened. How can I help you?'. They will want to cheer you up or make you laugh, especially when they see that you are down.

The Partner feels proud to be with you and socialise with your friends. Should they behave badly – because on occasion everyone can because no-one's perfect – they wouldn't try to justify or make excuses for their behaviour. Even when they don't share your passion for your hobbies and interests, they will at least show an interest and be supportive. Whether it is an upcoming test, an important interview or event, or a difficult time in your life, they'll 'be there' for you, cheering you on at the sidelines, rather than taking over and making the event about them.

The Partner is honest and straightforward: they don't play games with people's feelings. They respect you and your choices and want you to be happy. The Partner doesn't push you into things you don't feel comfortable with; they will want to get to know you before you have sex, rather than the other way around. The Partner will keep your confidence and wouldn't share your secrets because they care about you and love you and wouldn't want to hurt you. You can trust them and be relaxed around them.

The Partner can admit that they find things scary or when they have done something wrong. Most importantly, they will apologise when they do something you feel uncomfortable with and they won't do it again. They will take responsibility by saying, 'I'm really sorry that I . . . ', as opposed to 'I'm really sorry if you felt I . . . '. They certainly won't say that something was your fault when it clearly wasn't. Ultimately, they take responsibility for their own choices, language, actions and behaviours.

The Partner keeps good company. Generally, individuals are strongly influenced by a mixture of the people that surround them – friends (who you can choose) and family – so the Partner will probably have nice friends, too. And you're likely to get on with their friends well and feel safe around them.

The Partner respects people. You can tell how much the Partner likes women and/or men by the way they treat the key male and female figures in their life. They don't use their partner just for sex or for control: they don't believe that a person's gender or sexual identity should count against them. They don't make jokes at your expense or that make you or others feel uncomfortable.

In a relationship of love and respect, the Partner can be of any gender identity and whatever their sexual identity, the basic qualities of the Partner are the same.

Of course, there is no 'perfect' person out there – everyone has flaws and problems. But whereas the Controller might **say** that they like you and then treat you poorly, the Partner says they like you and **shows it to be true** in both their actions and their words.

LOVE IS
A DOING
WORD

WHAT DO YOU LOOK FOR IN YOUR IDEAL PARTNER?

Consider what your ideal partner would be like. Tick any of the following list that apply:

- [ ] An attractive face
- [ ] Physically fit and strong
- [ ] Has a twinkle in their eye or a cheeky grin
- [ ] Dresses and presents themselves well
- [ ] Popular
- [ ] Has a bit of a reputation - a 'bad' boy or 'sassy' girl
- [ ] Confident
- [ ] Commands respect from others
- [ ] Powerful and protective
- [ ] Clever
- [ ] Has a strong skill; for example, is good at football, plays in a band, is an artist
- [ ] Enjoys going out and has the money to do so
- [ ] Everyone likes them
- [ ] Comfortable in social situations
- [ ] Gets on with your family and friends
- [ ] Honest
- [ ] Straightforward
- [ ] Reliable
- [ ] Trustworthy
- [ ] Understanding
- [ ] Loyal

41

Now think about how your ideal partner would behave.
Tick any of the following list that apply:

☐ Takes you on a date or several dates

☐ Wants to explore new places or try new activities with you

☐ Buys you mementos from places where you go together

☐ Buys you gifts

☐ Walks you home or to and from school, college
or work to make sure you're safe

☐ Touches you gently and tenderly when holding and
cuddling you

☐ Shows you kindness and consideration

☐ Shows you affection

☐ Doesn't force you to do anything you don't want to

☐ Accepts that 'no' means 'no'

☐ Asks about your feelings

☐ Faithful

☐ Supports you in difficult situations

☐ Trusts you

☐ Respects your independence

☐ Likes and appreciates you and is able to tell you why

☐ Doesn't play games with your feelings

☐ Doesn't behave secretively

☐ Can admit to being wrong

☐ Respects your privacy, your space and
the person that you are

How would it feel to be in a relationship with your ideal partner?

Now that you've considered what you look for in a partner, let's think about how it would **feel** to be with this 'ideal' partner. Let's face it, you probably don't daydream about being with someone who is mean to you and makes you feel miserable! No matter who you are, you most likely want to feel good about yourself. It is an added bonus if feeling this good is connected to the person you are attracted to and are maybe in a relationship with. There would be nothing better than being able to be yourself when you're with them, because you would feel completely accepted, trusting, safe and relaxed.

The knowledge that you are in a relationship with someone who is demonstrating many of the dreamy and respectful behaviours identified above would give you a real experience of feeling secure and loved, and a sense of belonging. You would feel blissed out and special enough to be with the person you so admire. Perhaps this is the first glimpse of how you might imagine a grown-up and mature relationship to look.

43

A word of caution!

When you are attracted to a person who ticks all (or most) of your boxes, it is difficult to think that they would be anything other than amazing to be with. They seem almost 'perfect' and you imagine that you'd feel incredibly lucky to be with them! However, it is important to remember that even when a person presents themselves in an attractive way, **it doesn't necessarily follow that they will behave in an attractive way towards you**. As you proceed through the following chapters, you will learn that anyone can look like an ideal partner, but not everyone is. . .

Your Partner is their name.
Loving you **is in their nature.**

The Accepting Partner
- Accepts we have the right to end the relationship
- Believes we are an individual
- Can admit being wrong
- Respects our independence

The Caring Partner
- Respects us
- Is trustworthy
- Cares for us
- Is reliable

The Freedom Partner
- Encourages us to achieve
- Is nice to our friends
- Trusts us
- Is respectful of our family

The Loving Partner
- Hugs and kisses us
- Is faithful
- Accepts 'no' means 'no'
- Loves and appreciates us

The Supportive Partner
- Doesn't keep secrets
- Has a sense of humour
- Treats us as equals
- Compliments us

THE CONTROLLER

Chapter 3
THE CONTROLLER

Now that you've thought about what the ideal partner might be like, let's look at another type of partner: a controlling one. In this book, the term 'the Controller' is used to refer to this type of partner. This chapter looks at the different behaviours the Controller may employ to control their partner.

Who is the Controller?

The Controller will use a wide variety of behaviours, some of which may not appear to be particularly bad or abusive in the early stages of a relationship. Typically, they bombard and 'love bomb' you, rushing you into a whirlwind relationship, putting you on a pedestal to lure you into believing they are really into you. You might have met them in person, through a chance meeting or at a family event or through a friend. Alternatively, you may have met them online or been targeted or 'cherry picked' through your social media. **Reflecting on the context of how you meet a partner is very important in identifying the Controller.**

What does the Controller actually do?

The Controller can use one or several behaviours at the same time to coerce you into doing what they want you to do. In this book, five main 'characters' make up the Controller: the **Charmer (Chapter 4)**, the **Bully (Chapter 5)**, the **Mindmixer (Chapter 6)**, the **Taker (Chapter 7)** and the **Keeper (Chapter 8)**. Each of these different characters has their own set of behaviours and beliefs. The Controller can present as one or two of these characters or a combination of all of them.

Let's take an example:

Chantelle has arranged to meet her friends but at the last minute Darren calls saying he wants to see her. He persuades her to cancel her plans. The next morning, Darren suggests that Chantelle skips school so that they can spend more time together.

This could be seen as a loving gesture. Darren can't get enough of Chantelle; he wants to be with her every minute of the day. That is hardly the crime of the century, is it? Every now and then, in a healthy, loving and respectful relationship, you can probably imagine choosing to do either of these things with your partner rather than see your friends or go to school. However, it looks very different in the context of an abusive relationship.

If Darren encourages Chantelle to not see her friends or go to school because he wants her all to himself, it can seem super romantic and may make her feel really desired. But what if Chantelle wants to see her friends and insists that she is going to?

Darren sulks. He stops talking to Chantelle and stops returning messages. Chantelle worries about what he is thinking and why he is so upset with her. As a result, she focuses less on her friends and instead tries to make it up to Darren, so that he will start communicating with her again. It even puts her off seeing her friends because it isn't worth the fuss that Darren makes.

This is classic behaviour of the **Bully**. Alternatively, Darren might react like this:

Darren lies to Chantelle that one of her friends has said horrible things about her. Chantelle has it out with her friend, which creates a bad vibe and results in Chantelle and her friend not speaking to one another. Chantelle subsequently chooses Darren over the 'disloyal' friend and ends the friendship.

In this case, Darren has used a behaviour of the **Keeper**. Chantelle doesn't realise that he lied to her in the first place or that he has controlled her by stopping her seeing her friend. Clever, eh? When you have fewer friends, you can become more dependent on your partner to do things with and for company. This increases the opportunity for your partner to have more control over you.

Darren could have used a behaviour of the **Taker** to ensure Chantelle didn't want to go to school the next morning:

Whilst they are together one evening, Darren encourages Chantelle to allow him to take a semi-naked pic of her. However, he then threatens to send it to other people at school if she doesn't do what he wants.

In trying to persuade Chantelle to skip school Darren might use a behaviour of the **Charmer** and promise to take her out somewhere nice for the day or bribe her with a special gift. The lure of Darren doing something nice for Chantelle could appear to her as more inviting than controlling.

Alternatively, Darren might employ the behaviours of the **Mindmixer** and persuade Chantelle that she is wasting her time on her education, that she isn't smart enough and it's not worth her bothering because she won't get the grades she needs. Equally, he could use behaviours of the **Keeper** and perhaps hide her school bag, or adopt a behaviour of the **Bully** by trashing her books. However Darren actually behaves, Chantelle misses class either because she is promised a more exciting day, or because she is starting to feel mislead – downhearted that she isn't doing well in class so any enthusiasm she had for her studies has disappeared, or embarrassed because she doesn't have her books. Whatever the case, Chantelle ends up missing out on her education, which means she falls behind in class and might find it hard to catch up. If she continues to be influenced by Darren's controlling behaviours, over a period of time she may end up not going to school or college simply because she has lost all her self-confidence!

PLACES TO GET HELP

Childline provides information, advice and support – **tel: 0800 1111** or online chat and email via **www.childline.org.uk** If you are under 18 you can use the website to securely report nude/sexualised images to prevent them being uploaded: search for the 'Report Remove' tool and you will find clear instructions. When reporting in this way, it makes no difference whether you shared the image willingly or were coerced or groomed.

The Controller is their name.
Controlling you is in their game.

The Charmer
- Bribes us with gifts
- love bombs us
- Promises not to do it again
- Cries

The Bully
- Clenches fists
- Gives evil looks
- Hits us
- Sulks

The Keeper
- Tells us what to wear
- Follows us everywhere
- Stops us seeing friends
- Constantly texts us

The Taker
- Sends sexts
- Gets drunk or stoned
- Coerces us to have sex
- Flirts with our friends

The Mindmixer
- Laughs at us
- Humiliates us in front of others
- Puts us down
- Compares us to others

Can you identify any of the behaviours listed in the graphic on the previous page? If you are able to think of some additional behaviours, keep a note of them and see which character of the Controller they fit as you read on.

THE CONTROLLER

The Controller is their name, controlling me is their game...
They threaten you with words, they tightly clench their fist.
Your voice is never heard, yet they always say I'm missed.
They say they love me, but all they want is sex.
I know they're lying now, and their friends are taking bets.
I know I have to text them like 100 times a day,
And if I don't text back, I know I'll have to pay.
They cry a lot, yet I'm the one to blame.
They're charming me and have NO SHAME.

THE CHARMER

Chapter 4
THE CHARMER

The Charmer is one of the five different characters that the Controller adopts and is like a wolf in sheep's clothing. At the start of a relationship the Charmer will convince you that they think you are wonderful and that they are really into you, when they are actually luring you into a false sense of security. This would be identified as the grooming process, which is present at the beginning of all abusive relationships. The Charmer will then re-emerge at those times when you question the way they behave and/or when you want to end your relationship with them.

Nat and Izzy have recently started seeing each other after meeting through mutual friends. They have met up a couple of times on their own and Nat pays for everything. Nat is a Charmer, is super attentive, gives Izzy that cheeky smile, and pays her lots of compliments. Izzy can't believe how lucky she feels. One day when they go out, Nat treats Izzy to a couple of things – nothing expensive, but treats her to them all the same. A while later, they are in the park cuddling and chatting then Nat starts coming on a bit strong with Izzy, trying to kiss and touch her. Nat is trying to encourage Izzy to respond in the same way, but Izzy feels uncomfortable and wants Nat to stop. When Izzy manages to get Nat to stop, Nat switches behaviour and tells Izzy, 'I'm sorry, you're just so gorgeous I couldn't help myself'. Izzy feels flattered and believes Nat so they go back to having a cuddle. During this cuddling Nat changes approach and goes quiet, and doesn't speak much as they walk back to where Izzy lives. Izzy asks Nat what's wrong but doesn't get a response, leaving Izzy confused because Nat had been so attentive all day and now isn't speaking to her.

In this example, Nat has used the characters of the **Charmer** (taking Izzy out and treating her), the **Taker** (coming on a bit strong and getting sexual), and the **Bully** (giving Izzy the silent treatment because Nat didn't get his own way).

How Does The Charmer Behave Towards You?

At the early stage of a relationship, the Controller aims to make you believe that they are lovely, and that you're lucky they are interested in *you*. Get ready for the Charmer!

Best behaviour

If someone isn't nice to you when you first get together with them, you won't be particularly interested in having any kind of relationship with them. If they put you down, blame you for something you didn't do or make you feel stupid, it is unlikely to win you over! Therefore, at the onset of any relationship, everyone is on their very best behaviour – even you. For example, you probably resist farting or burping on first dates or the first few times you meet someone new.

It's similar to when people attend an interview for a place at college or for a job: they put on their best behaviour, wear something smart, get their 'look' right, maybe talk themselves up a bit, and some will stretch the facts about their behaviour and attitude to work. When a person wants something or someone, they generally focus on showing the best version of themselves to draw the other person's favourable attention towards them and get what they want.

The charm offensive

The Charmer makes their first impression on you by flirting, telling you the kinds of things you want to hear. As part of their 'charm offensive' they may say that you are just what they're looking for, that you are special, that they've never met anyone like you before, that they feel lucky to have met you

(even though they don't mean it), that you are gorgeous or good looking, 'fit', 'cool' or any other term designed to flatter you. They will make you laugh during the course of banter, laugh at your jokes and smile at you with that 'special' cheeky grin.

On the first few times you meet, the Charmer might take you out alone or invite you out with their friends, which can be enticing, particularly if they are a bit older than you. They might make promises such as to take you out then not actually take you anywhere, or about how they will treat you; for example, they might say they would never behave badly towards you or hurt you. When you're offered a promise at this early stage of getting to know someone who is so charming it can seem believable and therefore it's easy to be taken in by them.

The Charmer will likely be especially nice to your parents because the Charmer can charm parents too! They will probably get on well with your family and behave respectfully towards them, and may even tease you in front of them, which looks harmless because it is 'just' banter. When the 'joke' is at your expense and your family or your friends think your partner is funny and a 'laugh' there is already a danger that they have been fooled. Because your partner has won them over they might not necessarily see that you were the butt of the joke.

The **CHARMER** onscreen

The Charmer can be identified in almost every soap opera, TV drama and film. Such characters can persuade their partners or 'willing victims' to do anything – perhaps lured by a promise or a gift – and it looks utterly normal and, worse still, acceptable. James Bond is the ultimate Charmer: suave, handsome, slick, a glint in his eye, well turned out, oozing confidence and charisma, and always saving the day.

The giver of gifts

The Charmer might spoil you by buying you gifts – maybe clothes or a new mobile phone, jewellery or other things that you might not be able to afford for yourself or be old enough to buy, like alcohol or cigarettes. The Charmer may seduce you into their control by saying, for example:

'I'll get you **anything** you want.'
'You only deserve **the best**.'

Many prominent adverts are designed to instil the belief that when you receive a gift in a romantic context it's because you're special. Unless you are consciously aware of this influence, it can be too easy to believe that the reason the Charmer gives you presents is because they really like you. You may think that if they spend money on you or treat you, they must think highly of you – but where the Charmer is concerned, this is not necessarily the case as they will have an ulterior motive. When you are made to feel special by someone, you are more likely to view them positively and develop warm feelings towards them.

You have to ask yourself: Is the gift to genuinely treat me and make me feel special? Or was it given to make me feel indebted and to perhaps be used later as leverage when they want me to do something I don't want to do? If there is an expectation that you 'owe' them as a result of their gift, then they are indeed a Charmer. The thing they are most likely to want in return is to be sexual with you.

Love bombing

To experience 'love bombing' is a fantasy and should be treated with caution. The Charmer will 'love bomb' you, telling you that they love you and that you mean everything to them, that fate has brought you together and you are 'meant to be', and that they can't live without you. A whirlwind romance. Wow! Who wouldn't be delighted to hear someone say such lovely things to them? They may tell you:

'You're my **soulmate**.' '**You understand me**, better than anyone else.'

The Charmer builds you up and puts you on a pedestal. Once you are completely charmed and believe that they think the world of you, you feel 'loved up' and begin to invest your feelings in the relationship. You feel positive towards them, excited about the way they treat you and may even start to feel as if you love them. Once you are hooked in and are experiencing feelings towards them, your partner may start to behave as if they 'own' you – that you are theirs. Sometimes we too can behave in this way towards our partner.

Love songs

The Charmer might play you a particular song that has music designed to impact your feelings and lyrics saying that you should understand your partner better or you should try harder to make things work, even when it doesn't feel right, or that you should fight for your relationship, believe your partner's excuses about not being able to help what they do and so on. It is lovely to share a special song with the person you love but its sentiment will only ring true when you are in a non-coercive or non-abusive relationship. A special song will be played to affirm your togetherness in a loving relationship, and should not be confused with being used to coerce you into remembering how super attentive and 'loving' your partner was when you first met.

Charming online

You can also experience the behaviour of the Charmer online with someone you haven't met face to face. It is even easier for someone to be a Charmer online using dating apps and social media platforms. Whatever your gender or sexual identity, as a teenager you are finding your way with how you define yourself as well as the experience of new relationships. As part of this process, you may post information about yourself for others to see. When someone responds and seems to be into all the same things as you, shares the same

likes and dislikes as you and agrees with things you have put out there, it can feel awesome. But how do you know for sure that they are genuine? Even though they may appear to be too good to be true, with the good feeling that being validated brings it is even easier to be drawn in by someone online. Just as you can (or may have done), they may have edited their images and quite possibly do not at all look like them in reality. They may even be a totally different person who is posing as a teenager. People are often less inhibited online and you may be tempted to share things that you've never told anyone else with someone you have never met in person, simply because you have allowed yourself to believe you have something in common. See **Chapter 12**.

Take a step back

If you find yourself in the midst of a charm offensive and are feeling that this person is too good to be true, you should probably take this thought seriously and take a step back! You are in danger of falling for the Charmer because you 'want' what appears to be happening to be real – the fairy-tale romance or Disney love you see in films. You may have a niggling feeling not to trust what is happening or feel a bit pressured that things are going too quickly, but if you feel so loved up you may override the instinct or ignore your gut feeling. A rushed and speedy start to a relationship should always come with a warning.

'If it feels too good to be true, **it probably is**.'

PASSIVE AGGRESSIVE BEHAVIOUR

Passive aggressive behaviour tends to be subtle and can be difficult to see clearly. It involves acting 'indirectly aggressive' rather than 'directly aggressive'. A person may appear not to have an issue with something when in fact under the surface they hold very strong feelings about it but have no intention of being honest about this.

Passive aggression is a form of coercive control and it can trip you up and sabotage your plans. It prevents things from running smoothly: the abusive partner will literally create a problem and leave you to deal with the mess as if it is your responsibility. For example, your partner might appear to agree with you about an idea you have had or plans you have made with them, and they may even give the illusion that they are enthusiastic about your suggestion; but rather than going along with you and being co-operative, they deliberately go quiet, don't turn up on time, purposefully get it wrong, get angry with you about something else, become negative about the idea or plans, and/or generally resist you being able to succeed with your plan or idea.

The Charmer's passive aggressive behaviour

The 'sob story'

The passive aggressive Charmer will tell you a 'sob story' or 'poor me' story about their life that might have some truth in it, cleverly making themselves appear like the victim, and you may feel genuinely sorry for them. Examples of stories are: they are struggling with their situation at home; they are stressed; they have a 'problem' controlling their anger or feelings because of the way they have been treated themselves; or they have been diagnosed with a condition and need your support to get better or to change. In these stories the Charmer is never to blame – everyone else is responsible for why they feel and act the way they do. They may tell you:

'I've been **really** messed up by my family.'
'I've got **mental health issues**.'

This situation is difficult because at the onset of a relationship you don't know your partner well enough to discern if everything they tell you is true or not. If you've begun to have feelings for them you may see no reason to doubt what they say. However, if your partner claims that everyone else is responsible for why they feel the way they do, it is likely that **they will turn the tables on you and make you feel responsible for the way they feel**. You may even start to believe that you are to blame.

The blame laid on others in these stories are excuses for the Charmer's bad behaviour. For anyone to suggest that they have no responsibility for their behaviour would be a fib or a lie.

Everyone is responsible for their own behaviour and your partner doesn't have a right to punish you personally in response to feeling badly about themselves.

The Charmer will likely 'turn on the waterworks', crying in front of you. When someone cries following something you have done, you can easily assume that you have upset them. It can be so uncomfortable to witness someone crying that you will probably quickly give in and say you didn't mean what you said or shouldn't have done what you did. Observe how quickly they 'recover' and ask yourself if and how they've manipulated the situation.

Empty promises

As mentioned above, the Charmer might fail to see through a promise they have made to you or make excuses and consistently come up with reasons why they haven't done something, weren't available or couldn't meet you on time, or they might stall on things, and so on. However, at the same time they will give you every indication that they do want to do whatever it is you were hoping for, which is misleading and confusing – and, of course, disrespectful.

It is likely that the Charmer will then promise to change and say that in future they won't behave in certain ways as long as you are there for them and don't leave them. They might try to persuade you with:

'It will never happen **again**.'
'We are worth a **second chance**.'

Worse still, they may even make such promises to your family and try to charm and persuade them to believe what they are saying. Your family might be taken in and tell you that they think your partner is lovely and that you should be more supportive or understanding and give them a second chance, but **don't forget to listen to your intuition**.

When things don't go their way. . .

Once you start changing your mind about what you want to do because you're told you 'have' to or because your partner will threaten to punish you, hurt you or harm you otherwise, you enter the destructive dynamic of **coercive control** (see **Chapter 1**). In a relationship you should do things because you want to, not because you feel you have to or that there will be a negative consequence if you don't – that is not freedom of choice.

If you don't respond in the way your partner wants at this point, they could quickly change tactic: they may tell you a lie or blame you for everything that is wrong in your relationship, and because it's all your fault you should get help; or they may vehemently express that you are lucky that they put up with you! The passive aggressive Charmer can be quick to adjust their behaviour and mood when they don't get what they want from you.

How is The Charmer influenced to behave in this way?

Adverts are designed to influence and persuade us what to think and how to behave as well as to buy the products advertised. Every day we are bombarded with sumptuous adverts featuring romantic gestures of love to their partner with gifts of flowers, chocolates, cuddly toys, perfume and fragrances, designer clothing, jewellery, a mobile phone, alcohol, etc. They try to lure us into wishing that we are the person receiving the gifts in the advert! The imagery exudes the feel-good factor which a lot of people aspire to experience in their own relationships. The Charmer is seen to make these offerings to us by love bombing us in the first instance, or as an apology or to persuade us that they really do care about us. Under the influence of these adverts one could believe that being treated like this – albeit by the Charmer – is a good thing; and the Charmer may believe that mimicking the behaviour in these adverts is all they have to do to win you over and seduce you into the relationship. These adverts portray someone showering a partner or potential partner with gifts as being a normal and acceptable way to get what they want and that being persuasive in this way works.

It is not uncommon in adverts, films and dramas to feature 'kiss and make up' scenes where characters apologise or say 'sorry' and offer their gift. These characters appear to enjoy and make a big thing of the making-up process after a 'row'. It forces us to believe that we should all make a big effort

to make our relationship better and that working hard at the relationship will surely save it. This is an endless process though because we don't know what the end point is. When will our efforts be enough? The Charmer uses the gift as a way to get the last word, to persuade us to do what they want, to make us believe what they say or to stay with them. The Charmer always sets out to get their own way.

THE CYCLE OF ABUSE

The cycle of abuse is a way of describing how each abusive incident takes place. First, there is the **tension-building phase**, when you know something isn't right. You are walking on eggshells trying to please and placate (calm) your partner because you feel anxious and know something is going to kick off. As the tension builds it is likely to erupt into **crisis**; for example, an incident in which you are verbally threatened and insulted, your belongings are damaged or you are physically or sexually hurt and abused. Following crisis will come what is known as the **window of remorse**: your partner (the Charmer) will behave in a more loving and attentive way towards you. As a result, you start to feel more closely bonded to them and this is also known as 'reconciliation' or the 'honeymoon period'. The final stage of the cycle is **calm**, when your partner seems more co-operative and connected to you than usual, and you start to believe their behaviour was just a one-off. This period of calm can go on for days or weeks, until eventually you sense tension creeping in and the cycle begins all over again.

The cycle will repeat again and again, the period of calm getting shorter each time until there is no calm at all.

In the moment of crisis adrenaline is released, which is experienced as a strong surge of energy in the body. This hormone helps to mobilise a person for the 'fight or flight' response when they face a situation of threat: it heightens all their responses and lasts for up to an hour or until the threat/crisis decreases. Once the crisis point has passed, the senses remain heightened. If at that point the Charmer shows remorse by saying 'sorry' and they begin to demonstrate that they care, perhaps offering affection by touching and kissing you tenderly, all this will be experienced in a heightened way. This is why you hear people often describe the 'kiss and make up' moments as amazing, intense and passionate. (See pages 91 and 168 for further explanation of the 'fight or flight' response.)

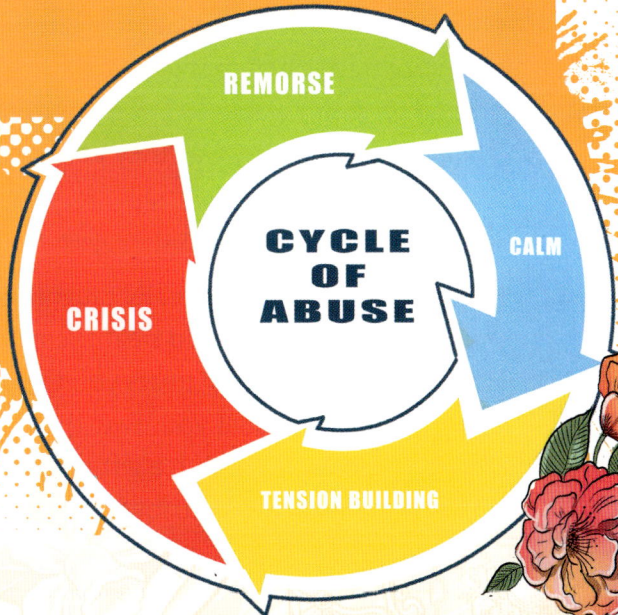

REMORSE

CALM

CYCLE
OF
ABUSE

CRISIS

TENSION BUILDING

It is not just in dramas with fictitious characters that we see what influences the Charmer, but in reality shows too. When a talent show or real-life documentary introduces the viewer to a person they are focusing on, usually they show how that person has overcome some adversity or difficulty in their life to get to where they are today. The idea of the backstory, or so-called 'sob story', in these entertainment programmes is used to appeal to the viewer's heart and emotions and create sympathy towards them. Of course, not everyone with a 'backstory' or a 'sob story' is trying to charm us and persuade us of something that is not real and true, but what this demonstrates more widely is the expectation that a so-called 'sob story' will appeal to our emotions and win us over.

This dynamic also happens when people who behave abusively in their relationship justify their behaviour by telling their partner their sob story, such as they have had a difficult time at home, something bad happened to them or they were bullied or mistreated in some way. Such justifications are often offered to their partner as a way of saying they couldn't help what they did and the way they behaved, and that it isn't their fault or responsibility. As you know, the Charmer believes you should accept the excuses they give.

In our society, we are generally taught that if someone treats you nicely then you should treat them nicely in return. However, if the Charmer treats you to something special, they might assume that you 'owe' them. For example, if the Charmer presents you with a gift or pays for a meal or a night out, you might believe you 'owe' them in some way.

It is **subtle**, but seemingly an acceptable way in which you are expected to treat the Charmer in return – perhaps in the form of a sexual favour.

These influences all send a message to the Charmer that they can get away with anything they want if they treat you to something nice or tell you they love you. They are also designed to make you feel sympathy towards your partner, to change your mind and keep going with your relationship.

WHAT DOES THE CHARMER BELIEVE ABOUT THEMSELVES AND THEIR PARTNER?

'I'm always right'

The Charmer believes that they are close to perfect. They think they are right and that nothing is ever their fault. When things aren't going their way, the Charmer will typically choose not to take responsibility for their own behaviour, so in their mind everything bad that happens to them is someone else's fault. Therefore, it is only logical to them that, as their partner, you are responsible for the way they feel and behave. The Charmer believes that they should be forgiven for everything they do and that you should just accept and believe the excuses they give for their behaviour. Consequently, they will think something is wrong with you if you don't believe everything they say to you.

'You're nothing without me'

The Charmer is big-headed and often has a high estimation of themself. They may believe that you are lucky to have them, are nothing without them and that you need them; they may also believe that they don't really need you. This is curious because if they see you in such a poor way and think so little of you, why are they with you?

The Charmer believes that they – and only they – have the right to end the relationship. They believe that launching a charm offensive against you will reel you in time after time, especially if they sense you are unhappy, needy or might want to end the relationship.

WHAT BELIEFS MIGHT YOU SHARE WITH THE CHARMER?

You might believe that you are really lucky to be with them because they could have chosen anyone, but they like you. You might also start to believe that it is up to you to make the Charmer happy, especially if they appear to be happy when they are with you. As your relationship continues, you might start trying to tease them out of a low mood or give them a lift if they appear down. If your focus is placed on them and making them feel better, before you know it, you might believe that they need you to care for them.

How Do you Feel When you aRe TReaTeD iN THiS Way?

Initially, it feels amazing to have someone who is so into you and loading on the compliments. You feel special and flattered to be the focus of their attention. In your early relationships it can make you feel grown up and respected. It is a very special feeling to have a partner regard you highly, especially when they are not part of your friendship group. When an independent person has picked you out – chosen *you* above everyone else – it can give you a sense of being wanted. In these circumstances, you can feel very loved, cherished and smothered with affection.

If the Charmer buys you gifts, you might believe you owe them somehow. You might feel you ought to do something for them in return, like a 'pay back'. You might believe they must really like you to treat you so nicely and at the early stages of your relationship when you are getting to know each other, you may see no reason why you would believe anything different. Caught up in the charm offensive, you can only consider that they are telling you the truth and are genuinely into you: it doesn't occur to you at this point that you may be being exploited for sex.

They can be very convincing, so at first you may be prepared to believe everything the Charmer says. You may be blinded by their charm and see no reason to doubt them. But as time passes and the novelty wears off, they will begin to pull you off the pedestal that they placed you on. From this

point onwards, you will experience upset. It doesn't make sense that you are being treated differently and you don't understand why you aren't feeling as cherished as you did at the beginning. Confused about the situation, you may not be able to work out what is real and true about your partner and the way they are behaving towards you.

If the Charmer starts to go back on the lovely things they initially said to you, it is likely to leave you feeling a bit duped, stupid and foolish. Because you can't make sense of what is happening, you can feel silly and a bit mugged off.

Ultimately, when you start to challenge your partner or try to make your own choices and they throw you a sob story in response, you can feel upset both for them and for yourself in the situation. You want to make a choice for yourself but are manipulated and coerced into feeling sorry for your partner for how your choice might impact them, and they may cry or threaten to hurt themselves. It is at this point that you can experience guilt to such an extent that you will easily retract and give up what you wanted for yourself and instead do whatever your partner wants. You are pushed into feeling the full weight of responsibility for your partner's wellbeing.

The situation will likely deteriorate to such an extent that you feel controlled and frightened of the consequences of the Charmer's threats and actions. Percieving yourself to be even more powerless, you can feel trapped in a situation you don't want to be in but are too scared to leave. You may sense danger or feel a bit cut off from it. This process is called being **desensitised**: it means you have become so used to the negative experiences and feelings you have that you don't see them for real or feel them anymore, and it is a **dangerous situation** to be in. Ultimately, you feel sad, miserable, exhausted and alone in the trap you are caught in. It can seem like you can't trust anyone with your feelings.

HOW TO GET HELP

If you identify any of the behaviours of the Charmer with your partner try and speak to a trusted friend or family member, or someone like a teacher, pastoral care or colleague who you feel you can trust, so that they can support you. It is important to recognise that you are not alone and there are people who care and can help. Contact one of the following helplines:

- **Childline** for information, advice and support – **tel: 0800 1111** or online chat and email via **www.childline.org.uk**
- See **'Places to Get Help'** (page 277) for a list of websites and helplines where you can get information and advice.

How Does The Accepting Partner Behave?

Unlike the Charmer, the Accepting Partner has genuinely good qualities. They like you and love you and don't want to change anything about you because they think that you are great just the way you are. They are kind and respect you and tell the truth. The Accepting Partner may disagree with you but can empathise with your feelings and will try to understand your perspective. They can take responsibility for their own behaviour, moods and feelings and don't seek to blame you for the way they feel – good or bad.

With the Accepting Partner you can have an equal relationship and work out difficulties together. When they buy you something, they don't expect anything in return; it is a kind gesture given with love not expectation.

The Accepting Partner likes your friends and family and doesn't try to stop you doing things with other people which don't involve them. They believe you have a right to your independence. You are free to pursue your goals and interests and are encouraged to do so. They support you to make your own decisions about what you want to do rather than persuade you to do something that they would prefer.

If you decide to end the relationship, they may ask for it to continue; however, once they realise that your decision is final they will – abeit reluctantly – accept it. They might even stay friends with you when the relationship has ended because they still like you as a person and what they liked about you hasn't changed.

THE BULLY

Chapter 5
THE BULLY

Bullies are everywhere in life, from the playground to the workplace, and sometimes they are even in the form of a family member or a friend. However, one of the places you least expect to be bullied is within your relationship. This chapter looks at the character of the Bully, one of the five different characters that the Controller adopts, and what it is like to be bullied by the person you love and who says they love you! Why would someone hurt you in any way if they care about you and/or love you?

Marcie and Sam have been seeing each other for a couple of months. Sam is known for being a bit badass and Marcie quite likes that Sam has a bit of a reputation. One afternoon Marcie's mum needed help, which meant Marcie had to change her plans with Sam. Sam gave the impression that it didn't matter and the two agreed to hook up later. Marcie went round to Sam's house in the evening and Sam seemed to be in a mood. Marcie tried to get out of Sam what was wrong but Sam wouldn't say, leaving Marcie second guessing what the problem must be. Sam just glared at her and gave her dirty looks, which made Marcie feel uncomfortable. When Marcie said she thought it was better for her to go home, Sam jumped up and stood in front of the door, blocking her exit. Sam verbally laid into her, telling her how she didn't care enough about their relationship and that other people seem to come first. Sam punched the wall and told Marcie she was lucky she didn't get hurt.

In this example, Sam has used the characters of the **Bully** (when Sam is moody, punches the wall and tells Marcie she is lucky she didn't get hurt), and the **Mindmixer** (when Sam spins round telling Marcie she didn't care about their relationship).

How Does The Bully Behave Towards you?

The Bully is perhaps the easiest character of the Controller to identify. One of the behaviours that the Bully makes a habit of is to always look 'angry' with you. This is a clever move on their part, as it can make you feel scared and therefore more likely to do as they say. There is little or no compromise or negotiation to be had with the Bully. They will always win the argument and you will always come off worse!

The Bully is good at using their voice to intimidate you. They might speak with a menacing tone or slow down their speech, talking to you sternly. They may even shout at you or spit the words at you. They might swear at you or threaten to harm you directly.

The Bully will tell you they know what is best for you and then apply pressure, coercing you to let them have control over decisions that should be yours, for instance saying:

'Do what I tell you **or else**.' ## '**Don't** make me mad.'

Because they look or behave in an aggressive or scary way towards you – for example, whispering or looking angry whilst making threats – you can feel that you have no choice but to do what they want as you are afraid of the consequences otherwise.

The Bully may use their friends to make life difficult for you, perhaps by getting them to intimidate and threaten you or to pester you; for example, by sending you mean and abusive texts through the night. This constant behaviour will increase your fear and vulnerability and may lead you to feel afraid to go out and live your life normally.

Getting physical

The Bully likes to create confrontation and may use body language to intimidate you; for example, squaring up to you and getting in your personal space, backing you into a corner, blocking your exit from a room, puffing up their chest and eyeballing you, or standing behind you or towering over you menacingly. They may have other significant aggressive behaviours that are designed to make you feel uneasy, like cracking their knuckles, tapping their foot or fingers, gritting their teeth, glaring at you or giving you evil looks and/or sly smiles.

The Bully may inflict all kinds of physical assaults on you – kicking, punching, hitting, slapping, choking, pinching, poking, pulling your hair, throwing things around, punching holes in the wall or door, smashing your mobile phone and personal belongings, pushing you into things – even in front of oncoming cars – and so on . . .

They could use absolutely anything as a weapon against you: for example, stab you with a knife, stubb out a cigarette on your skin, burn you with a pair of hair straighteners, or hit you with your mobile phone. Maybe they've even used their car to frighten you, by driving too fast, slamming on the breaks suddenly or banging the dashboard with their fists.

What do the Bully's passive aggressive behaviours look like?

Bullies are very good at mood swings – they can be nice one minute and nasty the next. They will switch on one mood or the other depending on what they want to achieve. Switching these behaviours on and off can be very confusing and unnerving. For example, the Bully might be very friendly towards you one minute and in the next, give you the silent treatment and say nothing at all, or sulk.

A common passive aggressive behaviour of the Bully is to not communicate at all when they have an issue or problem with your idea or plan. They might ignore you and avoid any discussion you might want to have. They might sulk, go silent, be miserable, sullen and negative in order to make you believe that there is a 'real' problem. They wouldn't let on that it is really a case of them feeling resentful and being determined to get their own way. You may then get so wrapped up in their 'real' problem that you might actually start feeling sympathy towards them. This passive aggressive behaviour actively steers you away from what you were trying to achieve and into doing what your partner wants. It is a very subtle form of coercion and manipulation.

The passive aggressive Bully might suddenly kick off for no apparent reason. It may appear to be unexpected and unprovoked, but one thing is for sure – you will be blamed for it! They may even push you into feeling angry and then turn the tables on you and make it look like you are the one with the 'anger' problem.

THE PASSIVE AGGRESSIVE WEB

How is the Bully influenced to behave in this way?

Society presents a multitude of influences for the Bully to feed on – for example, unsavoury characters in films and on social media postings – and also some people in their day-to-day life. A bullying partner may have witnessed their parent or carer being bullied or have been bullied themselves by a family member or someone else. When a person sees or experiences this behaviour from a young age, they can grow up to believe it is normal and may never question it. However, many people grow up with a dominant parent or bully and on the receiving end of coercive, controlling, aggressive and violent behaviours that in the home appear to be 'normal', but they do not go on to become abusive towards others in subsequent relationships.

Thankfully, this doesn't mean that all young people living with a bullying or aggressive parent will go on to bully their partners in relationships; indeed, the opposite can be true. In the same way, there are young people growing up in families with domestic abuse who don't go on to be victims in their own personal relationships.

Just like everyone else, the Bully will have experienced peer pressure and the need to conform to the same acceptable behaviours and gender roles of those in their friendship group or culture. In particular, teenagers who identify as male can feel driven towards 'macho' behaviours as a way of proving their 'maleness'. Guys who appear to be geeky, soft, caring and who don't have a strong physical presence can often be mocked. This gender stereotyping, i.e. the way that males and females 'should' look, is very prominent in mainstream films, TV dramas and adverts. For instance, soldiers and heroes are typically portrayed as 'hench', 'buff' or 'fit', implying that someone can't be a hero unless they have these traits.

TOXIC MASCULINITY

Toxic masculinity is a set of attitudes and behaviours stereotypically associated with or expected of men that are harmful to men, women and society as a whole. In many cultures, men are taught to be strong, to take risks, to be aggressive and to always want sex. They are encouraged to be superior, entitled, homophobic (a dislike or prejudice against people in gay relationships or who identify as LGBTQ+), misogynistic (to hate women), dominant and to bond with each other by humiliating people that they perceive to be vulnerable. Behaving in this way upholds the belief that you can't be a 'proper' man unless you act in this way. Males who don't conform to this standardised image are called names such as 'soyboy', 'wimp', 'nerd' or 'gay'.

By conditioning males to follow this code of conduct, society makes it difficult for them to be their authentic self, able to express normal, healthy emotions that all human beings have, whatever their gender. This is particularly difficult when a male is in an abusive relationship and/or experiences coercive control, sexual assault or trauma at the hands of their partner. How will they be able to talk about their experiences and express their feelings? Because society doesn't support men to identify, understand and nurture their full range of emotions, they can find it very difficult to deal with their feelings and as a result suffer from poor mental health, which is perhaps why there is a higher rate of suicide for males than for females. Society conditions males to be emotionally numb and lacking emotional resilience.

Society's tolerance of aggressive and violent behaviour influences the Bully. The way violence is portrayed in the news, books, films, TV dramas and games is sadly normalising it as a way of resolving issues and something to be expected. As people are exposed to more aggressive and violent behaviours – in person, in the media and onscreen – it is no surprise that more and more people resort to managing conflict and challenges in this way. It may also account for the increase in girls and young women using more aggressive and bullying behaviours. Some females will try out such behaviours with their partners and some may become the more dominant partner, either in the current relationship or a future one. Standing up for yourself and physically fighting back may work when you are younger, but for some it will continue to be the way they manage what happens to them. However, as females in heterosexual relationships mature into early adulthood, they are likely to come off worse as their male partner will probably be physically stronger and so able to overwhelm them.

The most popular video games have no strong females or nice guys who respect women. Some may justify this imbalance as it being simply a game and not real life; however, there is a lot of evidence to suggest that when young people play these kinds of games the content can have an adverse impact on the developing brain as well as on their belief systems.

WHAT DOES THE BULLY BELIEVE ABOUT THEMSELVES AND THEIR PARTNER?

Typically, the Bully believes that they have a right to control their partner, that they have some kind of ownership or a 'right of entitlement' over them; for instance, if their partner does something they regard as 'wrong', in their mind the partner deserves to be punished for it. The Bully knows that if they frighten you, you will be scared of them and by demonstrating their strength, you will understand how much they could hurt you physically. They may believe that it is acceptable to bully others to get what they want. They see no need for discussion or negotiation; they will simply coerce you without thinking twice about it. Bullies often believe that they are the dominant partner and that their partner is weaker – no matter the gender.

WHAT BELIEFS MIGHT YOU SHARE WITH THE BULLY?

If you are with someone who has the behaviours of the Bully, you probably like a bad boy or sassy, tough girl – someone who has a bit of a reputation for kicking off with other people. You may believe it is good to be with someone who seems strong on the assumption that they will look out for you and protect you. You may believe females are weaker than males, or that you are weaker than your partner. Whilst you may know that your partner has a reputation, you may also believe that they would never behave in that way towards you.

You like someone who takes control and to be in charge of what happens in your relationship. If you are persuaded that you did something wrong, you might believe that you deserve to be punished. Some people have the belief that if their partner doesn't punish them, they aren't that bothered about them, i.e. they would only punish you because they care. This is a myth. **A partner only hurts you because they choose to; it is never because they care about you.**

Shockingly, about 80 per cent of young people will stay in a relationship with their partner after the first hit, slap or punch. It can be confusing but typically, if your partner physically hurts you they will give a reason why they did it and persuade you that it is valid, even though they will also tell you it was your fault. However, the truth is that your partner has made a choice to behave in this way. Over time you may become desensitised (i.e. so used to the negative experiences and feelings that you don't see them for real or feel them anymore) and believe that violence in a relationship is a normal consequence when you do something wrong. The grip of the Bully's control is very strong and overwhelming.

It is quite common for the abused partner to believe that the Bully behaves the way they do because they have low self-esteem. For some, that may be the case; however, many bullies are not insecure. They have a high sense of entitlement and believe they have the right to behave any way they want to, to be in control. They may have you believe otherwise, but they don't care about your feelings.

The Way You Make Me Feel

I have always been terrified of your dominating ways.
I don't know how much longer I can stay sane.

You never seem to care about the way I feel.
All I want is to be happy and enjoy a meal.
You've never loved me although you say it all the time.

I keep a smile, so you don't think I'm weak
But smiling is the only way to get me through the week.

How Do You Feel When You Are Treated In This Way?

In the company of the Bully you are likely to feel frightened and even sick with fear about what will happen next, especially if they hurt you or you felt you were going to die. You might not get any rest or be able to sleep because the level of fear, nervous tension and anxiety you experience means you are constantly braced ready for action, in the 'fight or flight' response.

The 'fight or flight' response, also known as a stress response, enables you to react quickly and appropriately to a stressful or life-threatening danger so that you can survive it. This survival instinct triggers the release of adrenaline, a hormone to help mobilise you towards **fight** – when you hit out or try to stand up to the danger or fear, in an attempt to stop what is happening – or **flight** – when you run away or try to escape from the situation. It is like a surge of energy to help you cope in a situation in which you feel nervous or scared about what is happening or will happen next. (See illustration below and page 168 for further explanation of the 'fight or flight' response.)

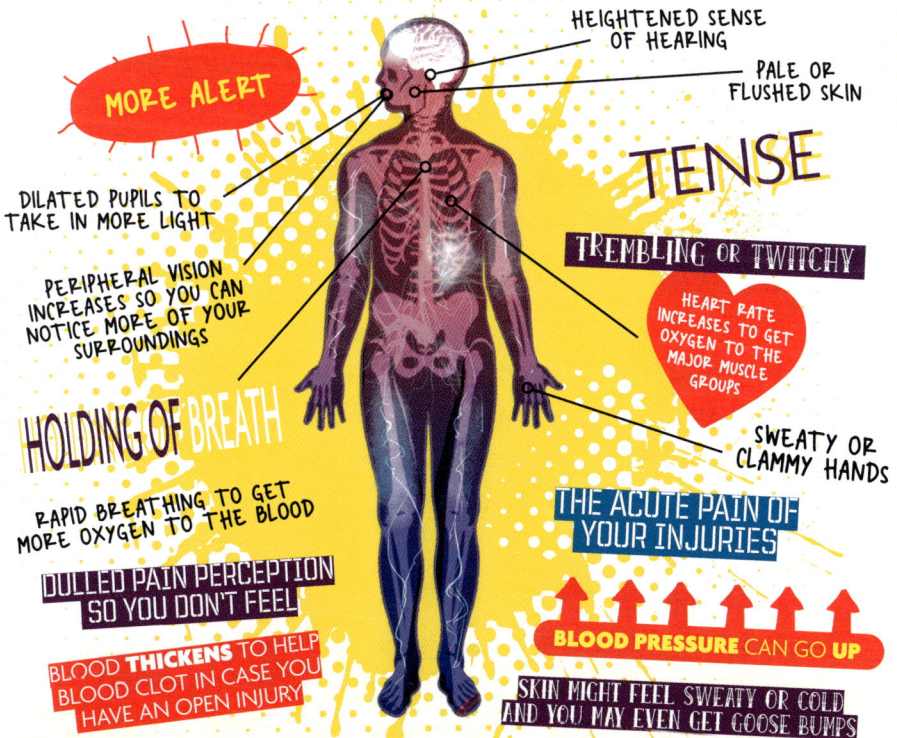

MORE ALERT

HEIGHTENED SENSE OF HEARING

PALE OR FLUSHED SKIN

DILATED PUPILS TO TAKE IN MORE LIGHT

TENSE

PERIPHERAL VISION INCREASES SO YOU CAN NOTICE MORE OF YOUR SURROUNDINGS

TREMBLING OR TWITCHY

HEART RATE INCREASES TO GET OXYGEN TO THE MAJOR MUSCLE GROUPS

HOLDING OF BREATH

SWEATY OR CLAMMY HANDS

RAPID BREATHING TO GET MORE OXYGEN TO THE BLOOD

THE ACUTE PAIN OF YOUR INJURIES

DULLED PAIN PERCEPTION SO YOU DON'T FEEL

BLOOD PRESSURE CAN GO UP

BLOOD **THICKENS** TO HELP BLOOD CLOT IN CASE YOU HAVE AN OPEN INJURY

SKIN MIGHT FEEL SWEATY OR COLD AND YOU MAY EVEN GET GOOSE BUMPS

After you have experienced a frightening or traumatic incident, or a pattern of such incidents, at the hands of the Bully, your body can begin to develop an exaggerated stress response. It is hard to live with this repeated stress response and it can have a damaging impact on your physical and mental health. As a consequence, you can begin to feel less and less like yourself, and after a while you may forget what it is like to be your normal self. You can experience a recurring pattern of response, whereby you anticipate something bad happening to you at any minute, which then triggers and activates the stress response, creating a habitual pattern of response. This is known as being hyper-vigilant and over-watchful. **Examples of triggers are: hearing a loud bang, a door being slammed, someone shouting at you, hearing others arguing, tense atmospheres or someone glaring at you or giving you 'that' look – there are many others.**

Of course, if the bullying you experience involves physical abuse or assault, once you are out of immediate danger, you will feel the hurt and pain of your bruises and maybe even find yourself in emotional shock. This could take the form of: feeling jittery, being sick or feeling as if you might vomit, being foggy headed, not being able to think straight, experiencing a tightness in your chest, feeling vulnerable, being disconnected from the experience you have had, feeling numb and/or being in a state of disbelief.

If your partner attends the same school or college as you, you may not want to go there as it is the only way to escape being with them. And if they have used their friends to bully you,

you will be even more scared. In this situation, you might feel alone and isolated and as if nobody likes you, and start to feel lost and as if things are spiralling out of control. You may not wish to tell anyone, perhaps because you feel ashamed and/or are too scared to tell anyone because you fear what your partner might do if they find out. By keeping these feelings inside you they are likely to intensify; in particular, the feeling of anger will grow because you aren't safe to express it to the Bully. Even though you may not acknowledge your anger as such, one thing you do know is that it's a big feeling to carry around! Anger expresses itself in different ways; for example, you can become spikey and defensive with others, especially those closest to you. It may be such a strong and overwhelming feeling that you act aggressively and are hurtful towards others, maybe even using bullying behaviours yourself.

When your partner uses passive aggressive behaviours like sulking or going silent on you, you can spend a huge amount of time trying to work out why they are behaving like that and questioning what you did that was so wrong to deserve this kind of behaviour. This is tiring and can wear you down, and it certainly distracts you from focusing on yourself and the other impacts the Bully's behaviour is having on you. By giving all your attention to them, you neglect your own needs. You can feel confused and upset that you may have done something wrong. Once you start to believe that it must be you who is doing things wrong, you can feel guilty, stupid and frustrated.

The effects of the Bully's behaviour are likely to lead you to feel sad, helpless, desperate, crushed as if the very core of you has been destroyed and sent you out of control, and you may cry yourself to sleep. You can feel afraid of getting things wrong in front of the Bully in anticipation of being punished and hurt. You may feel useless because you are repeatedly being told that it is your fault you are being punished because you can't get things right. Consequently, you might feel hateful towards yourself. In extreme cases, this can lead to self-harming (see 'Self-harm' box on page 165). You can feel the need to punish yourself for being angry about what is happening to you, but too scared or without the inner strength to stop it. You may feel at times like you just want to escape or stop the painful feelings. For some victims of bullying this may escalate to having suicidal thoughts.

The feelings described here are normal responses to being treated abusively by the Bully; but it doesn't mean that you have to put up with this behaviour and continue with the relationship.

ANGER

Anger is a strong, healthy and normal emotion which is often referred to negatively, because of the way it is expressed. Most commonly, anger is associated with big destructive outbursts which are threatening, aggressive, verbally abusive and/or violent. Anger is generally activated in response to feeling attacked, unfairly treated, ignored, deceived, or when facing a situation of injustice or disempowerment.

However, the emotion of anger is hugely important as it tells you clearly how strongly or passionately you feel about an issue or concern. For example, you can feel angry about misogyny, homophobia, racism, inequality, the way a friend or family member is being treated, climate change, cruelty to animals, and passionate about making a change or a difference based on your beliefs. Anger can drive you towards change and meeting your goals.

Anger affects everyone differently. For example, you can respond defensively and/or be the first to attack the other. Sometimes anger can be your default response – your go-to emotion because you don't want to feel the discomfort of the primary emotions of sadness and fear. You can learn to block those emotions out and only present with anger because it maintains distance from your own emotional pain.

Alternatively, in this context, when you are in a controlling and abusive relationship, you may well not feel safe – for whatever reason – to express your sadness, fear or anger and instead turn the anger inwards as if you are having a go at yourself. You deny yourself pleasure, comfort and connection with others, cutting yourself off from family and friends, and telling yourself hurtful and negative things – you are bad, useless, unlovable, hateful, stupid, pathetic, etc. Turning anger inwards like this can have a serious impact on your mental health and can lead to depression, self-harm (see 'Self-harm' box on page 165), and/or substance or alcohol misuse.

ANGER (continued)

You may recognise some of the physical signs of anger for yourself – tense muscles, rapid heartbeat, tightness in the chest, feeling hot, being nervous, the body shaking or trembling, having sweaty palms and being unable to relax. Along with the physical experience of anger you may feel resentful, hurt, humiliated, shamed or guilty.

HOW TO GET HELP

If you are feeling like you want to harm yourself or are having suicidal thoughts, it is important that you ask for help right away. Do not delay contacting one of the following helplines:

- **Childline** provides information, advice and support – **tel: 0800 1111** or online chat and email via **www.childline.org.uk**
- **Samaritans** provide a 24-hour helpline if you feel in crisis – **tel: 116 123**
- **Young Minds Crisis Messenger** – **text: YM** to **85258** (free)
- **The Mix** offers email and webchat support to under 25s – **www.themix.org.uk**
- **Papyrus** offers support to young people struggling with suicidal thoughts – **tel: 0800 0684141** or **text: 07860 039967**
- **CALM** provides support to anyone in the UK who is feeling down and needs to talk or find information to help with their situation – **tel: 0800 585858** or visit **www.thecalmzone.net**
- **Calm Harm** is a **free app** that provides resources for when you want to hurt yourself.

Sleepless Nights

I sometimes lie awake and wonder why
I follow step by step their rules that apply
Making sure I do my best to keep them happy
Keeping them pleased is the only way
If not, they will make me pay
It may be a slap, a punch or a kick
I really thought I'd never be hit
All these emotions going through my head
This is what it's come to being scared in my bed

IN
A WORLD WHERE
YOU CAN BE
ANYTHING
BE KIND

How Does The Caring Partner Behave?

The opposite of the Bully, the Caring Partner treats us with respect. They have a friendly nature and care about others — they may even care about people they don't know who face difficult times or hardship.

The Caring Partner doesn't believe in using violence to get their needs met. They might fight back if attacked by someone else, but they don't go looking for trouble with others as they don't need to prove themselves in that way. They are gentle and kind with you as well as with other people. They might even be protective of your needs and feelings, as well as of the feelings of others.

The Caring Partner doesn't snatch things from you and is careful with your belongings, treating you and your possessions with respect. If they make a mistake or wrongly judge something, they will admit they are wrong and won't look to blame you or anyone else for the mistake they made. They can take responsibility for their own actions.

The Caring Partner communicates what they think and feel and discusses their ideas with you. They talk about things. Better still, they are always ready to listen to you. You might not always agree, and you may see things differently, but you can agree to have different opinions. The Caring Partner doesn't try to keep persuading you to agree with them until you give in! Best of all, they smile at you and are affectionate. They don't sulk as a means to get their own way and make you feel bad.

THE MINDMIXER

Chapter 6
THE MINDMIXER

The character of the Mindmixer is one of the five different characters that the Controller adopts. This character will play mind games with you to such an extent that you can find it difficult to keep a grip on what is actually happening. Bit by bit, the Mindmixer will chip away at your sense of self, how you think, and how you look until you feel completely dismantled, broken and lacking the confidence to trust your own judgement.

Millie and Tara have been hanging out together at school as an item for nearly four months. They are in the same sets for a few of their subjects and sometimes study together after school. When Tara received a lower mark than usual in a test, Millie offered reassurance: 'It's okay, everyone gets things wrong sometimes.' Tara assumed that Millie was being supportive and understanding; but later when Tara asked something, Millie replied: 'Don't be so dim.' Although she said it with a smile on her face, it was confusing for Tara: it looked like Millie was teasing but it felt more hurtful than that. This escalated to Millie making constant snipes about anything Tara did such as 'What's got into you?', 'You're really letting yourself down', and 'You'll end up in the bottom set if you carry on like this'. When Tara accused Millie of being mean, Millie was told to stop being so over-sensitive. The following day, Millie took a pic of Tara, making a joke about Tara's hair in front of their friends and then posted it with a comment. Tara would normally have laughed this off but instead felt stupid in front of everyone. Later, on the way home, Tara tried to tell Millie how those comments had hurt. Millie behaved as if she were completely surprised saying: 'How could you think that of me?'. Millie continued: 'You know, you are quite hard work, Tara. I'm tired of you relying on me and then accusing me of being mean. You're lucky I've been there for you. Nobody else would be.'

In this example, Millie clearly demonstrates the character of the **Mindmixer**.

How Does The Mindmixer Behave Towards You?

Chipping away at you

The **Charmer** will put you on a pedestal at the beginning of your relationship, with comments designed to make you feel great and boost your confidence. But the **Mindmixer** will pull you off that pedestal through a gradual process of putting you down and dismantling your sense of self, i.e. who you are as a person and how you see things. Once that is achieved, it is easier for the **Controller** to use all of their behaviours to establish full control over you.

The Mindmixer focuses their abuse on the personal, making comments about the way you think, look and behave. They might say things like:

'**You** look a state.'

'You'll show me up looking **like that**.'

'You could **make a bit more effort**.'

After a time, this could escalate to a point where you begin to believe them more than yourself. If this happens you may, for instance, feel like making radical changes to the way you look, especially if they make specific comments such as:

'You'd look **really hot** if you got your boobs done.'

'You should **get your nose made smaller**.'

'You should **work out more**.'

'You'd be really attractive **if** you were blonde.'

If they perceive that you are susceptible, the Mindmixer might tell you that your hair is a mess and would look nice if you had it cut shorter or if you grew it longer or that you're looking tubby or fat, or even ugly! This may lead you to become more self-conscious than before and to consider a strict diet which almost certainly isn't healthy for you. When you start changing things about yourself in order to satisfy your partner, you are being coerced by the Mindmixer.

The Mindmixer is very good at offering their opinion on what you look like in comparison to other people, particularly air-brushed celebrities. They may also compare you to your friends or, worse still, their ex! They might even tell you that they fancy these other people, implying that you aren't good enough as you are. From this, you may be forgiven for believing that you need to make some changes to the way you look in order to be more acceptable to them, and to avoid their criticism. Not so!

Some of this may be said in front of other people and, for maximum impact, may be posted on their social media – like that really embarrassing photo of you where you were talking, but the shot captured you mid open mouth with a weird look in your eye (and highlighted the big red pimple on the end of your nose. . .). When it comes to laughing at you, embarrassing you and humiliating you in front of your friends and others, the Mindmixer doesn't know when to stop.

The Mindmixer trips you up at every opportunity, dismantling you bit by bit. They plant seeds of doubt in your mind about yourself by saying things that seem normal but are sure steps towards undermining you; for example, 'You're being silly', 'You're an idiot', 'You shouldn't be so stupid', 'You don't know what you are doing', 'You can't get anything right', and so on. When you challenge these comments or try to express your feelings the Mindmixer might tell you that you're being a bit over the top, too sensitive, ridiculous, unreasonable, annoying, or that you are 'mad', 'losing it', 'unhinged' or 'fucked up'.

The Mindmixer may take or hide your things – keys, mobile phone, books, personal or sentimental possessions – and then lie, saying that they haven't. Or they'll make out that they've told you things when they haven't; for example, 'I told you the other day – can't you even remember that?', 'You're so forgetful' or 'You're going mad'. Indeed, they could easily lie to you about absolutely anything and everything.

Negging

In order for these comments to land successfully with you, the Mindmixer will dress them up as a bit of a joke and deliver them with a smile or a cheeky grin. This makes it tricky for you to work out whether they are genuinely joking with you or are being serious. It is confusing when someone insults or reduces you in some way *and* has a smile on their face. Your brain tells you that because they're smiling it isn't serious, but the content of the comment puts you down and diminishes you, making you feel badly about yourself. Either way, you can't work out whether the comment was meant as a joke or not and this can create an experience of self-doubt, which does your head in: this is known as **negging**.

A 'neg' is a light insult disguised as a compliment. It is also known as a backhanded compliment, crack, cut, dig, insult, joke, jibe, parting shot, put-down, scoff, slam, snappy comeback, snub, take-down or taunt. For example:

Straightforward compliment: 'You're gorgeous.'

Neg: 'If you smartened yourself up and did your hair differently, I might be prepared to be seen with you in public.'

The negging comment is designed to diminish or reduce you in some way. Have you ever found yourself in a situation where someone coming on to you was rude because you didn't respond in the way they wanted you to? For example:

> **When someone calls you 'high maintenance, but attractive' before asking you out, and then when you turn them down, they insult you.**

> **As a girl walks across a car park towards the train station, a group of guys shout out: 'Oi, posh, come over here', 'Hey, sexy', and so on. Being alone, she feels intimidated and doesn't look in their direction. As the girl walks past them, the comments change to: 'Think you are better than me?', 'What the fuck?', and then 'Fucking slag', 'Snobby bitch' and 'I was only fucking joking, slut. You ain't worth it'.**

These two examples demonstrate how a person makes a negative judgement – i.e. 'high maintenance' and 'oi posh' – to draw your attention to them. It is done as if you should be grateful, not only for what they have said, but for their approval and for them making the effort to talk to you. This behaviour is often associated with trying to pick someone up or early dating.

The bottom line is that there's no legitimate, valid or sane reason why anyone should neg you. They may be giving you attention, but it is not the same as a compliment. You aren't getting lucky and, more importantly, **you don't need to tolerate it**. All behaviour forms a context, and this kind of attention should be a red flag to you. Walk away. Move on.

Sharing your secrets

You might have told your partner some things about yourself that you've never spoken to anyone else about – secrets, bad times, bad dreams, insecurities, fears and all of the other things you worry about. This is natural in a healthy relationship when you are learning about one another and developing trust. However, in a relationship with the Mindmixer you might find that your secrets, fears and insecurities are exposed to others on social media, to friends and even family members. Having your deepest thoughts and feelings put out there for all to see has maximum impact: not only have they exposed you, but others will make comments and have their say about your personal stuff too. Social media is a means to communicate instantaneously to the masses – well, at least to everyone you know now and may know in the future! In terms of humiliation, it is a wonderful weapon for the Mindmixer to use.

You don't have to tell your partner everything about your life. It's okay not to tell them about private and personal experiences in your history, even if you feel pressured to share things before you're ready. Sometimes you may think you should 'tell all', but that would put you in the vulnerable position of **hoping** for trust in a relationship **before** establishing that the other person is worthy of your trust.

For example, a 'friend' might threaten to expose a deeply personal piece of information such as your sexual identity, something that is a big deal for a young person if they haven't yet come out to their family. Coming out as gay is a personal choice that should be theirs and theirs only, but could be denied to them by the Mindmixer or used as leverage to coerce them.

Gaslighting

The Mindmixer will manipulate and confuse you into believing whatever they want you to believe, more commonly known as 'gaslighting' or 'crazymaking'. Put simply, the abusive partner will play games with your mind, making you feel stupid for feeling confused and causing you to worry that you are going mad. For example, they may tell you they didn't say what they did say; they didn't laugh at you when they did; they didn't put you down when they did; they didn't compare you to others when they did; and didn't call you names when they did.

'It's all **in your head**.'

GASLIGHTING

The term 'gaslighting' is used to describe psychological manipulation and abuse that makes you question whether you can actually rely on yourself. The term comes from a play called *Gaslight* that was performed in 1938, in which the husband tries to convince his wife, and the other characters, that she is mad and has no grasp on reality. When he dims the gas lights, he insists to his wife that she is imagining it.

There are typically three stages in the 'gaslighting' process: **idealisation**, **devaluation** and **discard**:

IDEALISATION: In the first stage, also known as the 'grooming' stage, the Charmer is in their element – they put their partner (the victim) on a pedestal, making them feel as though they are wonderfully adored, behaving in an overly affectionate and seemingly nice way. It may feel good at the time, but it's all a pretence.

DEVALUATION: In this stage, the victim is, almost without realising, pulled off the pedestal by the Mindmixer – they find that they're no longer adored, but instead are treated as if they're incapable of doing anything right. Sadly, because they've experienced and enjoyed the lovely behaviours in the first stage, they may think that if they work really hard things will get back to the way they were. They believe it is their responsibility to put things right and make the relationship better.

DISCARD: In the final stage, the victim is rejected and dropped. The abusive partner is likely preparing for the idealisation stage of the next victim.

If these experiences resonate, consider that you are having a lucky escape and should absolutely let your partner go! The confusion and rejection experienced by the victim can be very difficult to come to terms with.

Blaming your hormones

If you menstruate (have periods), another typical way in which the Mindmixer can persuade you that something is your fault is to blame your hormones. For example, if you try to clarify something that might have just happened, the Mindmixer might say:

'You must be **mid-cycle**.'

'You always get lairy **when you are on**.'

'**I can't take you seriously** when you are due on.'

The very clever thing about the hormonal cycle being used against you is that for some the reality is that they don't feel quite like themselves at particular times in their monthly cycle. Feeling a bit vulnerable is a common experience for those who menstruate – of all ages – just before their period. The hypothalamus, located in the brain, controls the hormones in the body, including all those involved in the menstrual cycle. Young people who menstruate, especially, can feel very disconcerted because often they don't understand the power of hormones and how, in relation to their periods, they are pretty much out of their control. When you are feeling a bit out of sorts, it is easy to be drawn in to believe that you are over-reacting, over-sensitive, being silly, over-emotional and irrational – even a bit mad! In this temporary state, you may conclude that, somehow, you got it wrong, didn't hear properly, must have misunderstood or been over-sensitive. When you experience pre-menstrual tension (PMT), it is not uncommon to judge things slightly differently and therefore it is easily used as a weapon by those who do not have periods. Equally, if you are using any medication to adjust your hormones, like the contraceptive pill or undergoing hormone replacement therapy (HRT), this, too, can be used against you.

Three types of lie

An abusive partner will tell you many lies in the course of your relationship and this is part of the pattern of abuse behaviour. If you are unlucky enough to hook up with an abusive partner, be aware that they will lie to you constantly. These lies make you question the reality of your experiences and are part of the process of dismantling your sense of what is happening, what is true and what is wrong in your relationship. There are three main types of lie – denial, minimisation and blame – and the Mindmixer can use each to throw you off kilter and convince you to believe it is a failing of yours that you 'feel' hurt, rather than a **fault of theirs** for behaving abusively towards you.

Denial: This is when the Mindmixer denies having said something to you when they have, or states that they can't remember what they have done to you, when it clearly isn't the case.

This leaves you remembering and knowing what happened to you, but wondering if you imagined it, which is confusing and frustrating.

Minimisation: This is when the Mindmixer reduces your experience of everything. 'It was only a joke.' 'It was just a bit of bants.' 'I didn't hit you that hard, it was only a slap.' 'It was just a bit rough.' 'It was nothing.' 'You are over-reacting.' 'You exaggerate everything.' 'You're so over-sensitive.' In this way, all the unkind, uncomfortable and painful experiences you have at the hands of the person who is meant to care about you and even love you, are made out to be less than they are. It's like your experience of what happens to you doesn't count for anything. Your experience is reduced, put down, diminished and discarded. Confused, you may begin to believe your partner's take on things, and start believing that you are losing your grip and not seeing things clearly. Further, you may start to think of yourself as a bit of a mess and believe that nobody else would put up with you.

Blame: The Mindmixer will blame you for saying or doing something wrong, or for not doing what they expect you to do. 'If you hadn't behaved in that way, I wouldn't have hit you.' 'If you had listened to me in the first place, things wouldn't have got out of control.' 'You made me so angry, I just lost it.' 'It's your fault.' 'It's because I love you that I do these things.' 'It's not my fault you bruise so easily.' It's disturbing to consider that the Mindmixer will blame their partner for everything, as if they have no control whatsoever over their own behaviour. They behave in this way because they don't care about their partner and are confident that they have all the power and control in the relationship. However, if you believe that you love this person and want to make things right, you will try harder even though you actually have no power in the relationship.

The Mindmixer is at play in *all* abusive relationships and gets to the very core of you. If you have been emotionally dismantled and pulled apart, it is much easier for them — and/or other abusers — to use other forms of abuse against you.

'We have been through so much together and most of it was **your fault**!'

WHAT DO THE MINDMIXER'S PASSIVE AGGRESSIVE BEHAVIOURS LOOK LIKE?

Keeping you on your toes

The Mindmixer uses passive aggressive behaviours like being unclear or vague about what they mean and never being directly open and honest about what they are thinking. Often, they will choose not to tell you what they are doing or what their plans are, so you never really know what they are up to. This keeps you on your toes, guessing and **focused on them**! This secretive behaviour tells you that you aren't important enough to them to be kept in the loop.

They might regularly turn up late and tell you that you got the time or place wrong or, worse still, stand you up and leave you waiting for them. When you call or message them to check what is happening, they don't answer. If you wait for a long time and even worry whether something bad has happened to them, all your attention will be focused on them — even when they aren't with you, they're in control! This is a very obvious way to demonstrate disrespect towards you.

Avoidance

On the surface, the passive aggressive Mindmixer may appear not to have an issue with something; however, under the surface the reverse may be true, but they have no intention of being honest about this with you (see 'Passive aggressive behaviour' box on page 63). For example, they will drag their feet to stall things, take their time, or make excuses to put off whatever it is that bothers them. All these tactics are designed to prevent something from happening that involves you or failing to see through on a promise they have made to you, because right from the start they had no intention of doing what they told you they would. Classic passive aggressive behaviours of the Mindmixer are to roll their eyes at you when you're talking about something that's important to you or looking at you in a dismissive way to suggest that what you are saying isn't that big a deal.

Making fun of you

The passive aggressive Mindmixer uses what looks like humour to fool you into thinking that they are 'only' joking. They achieve this by making fun of the things you like, the things you say, your ideas, your dreams, aspirations and opinions. They may directly tell you that you're being silly and unrealistic: 'Are you that stupid?' or 'I knew you were thick, but you are taking the mick now'. They might directly laugh at you, the things you say, achieve, succeed in or create. They may even call this sarcasm. When a person laughs *at* you, you may confuse this as laughing *with* you and think that they don't really mean it, passing it off as 'just' heavy-duty teasing, a bit of banter and perhaps you need to lighten up and get a sense of humour! They may actually tell you they are 'just' teasing you or winding you up a bit. You can accept that 'just teasing' is found in lots of happy and sorted relationships; but when it is coupled with some of the other aspects of the Mindmixer you need to consider the context of your relationship more carefully. One thing is for sure with the Mindmixer: if you dared to tease them in a loving way, whether on your own or in front of friends, they wouldn't see the funny side and would likely punish you in some way for it.

It is the same principle when your partner makes fun of or belittles your achievements. The things you do and achieve are uniquely part of you and help to define who you are, what you feel and what you stand for. If anyone puts you down by chipping away at you like this, they are attacking the very core of you, your self-esteem – how you see yourself. They may also use sexist or racist jokes directed at you personally, using your gender, race, age, sexuality or difference to hurt your feelings and generally insult you. How you see yourself will have a direct impact on how you feel about yourself (see **Chapter 11**).

Being teased is usually something done in jest and with good humour, and you may also find it funny. However, when you tell your partner that what they said isn't funny from your perspective or that it upset you and they continue to say similar things to you, their behaviour becomes abusive.

Name-calling

The Mindmixer never calls you by your actual name.
Initially they may call you babe, baby, bae, peng, sweets,
wifey, princess, sexy, gorgeous, fit, and so on. However, at some
point, alongside putting you down, they might start using
derogatory language. Girls might hear words like skank, slut,
stupid bitch, slag, skettel, bimbo, airhead, tart or ho, while
guys might hear put-downs such as pussy, wimp, pansy, ape or
soyboy. For people who have changed their gender identity,
and thereby wish to be known by a different name,
the Mindmixer might purposefully choose to use their birth
(now dead) name, commonly known as 'deadnaming'.

When the name-calling starts, you might not even notice
because it will be put across like it's a joke or you may even
mistake it for affection. If the Mindmixer smiles when they
call you names, you may think they're teasing you because they
don't look serious. However, the name-calling will increase and
soon the names you are called will not be said in fun or jest.

Moving the goal posts

The Mindmixer may appear to change their mind all the
time, which is commonly known as moving the goal posts
or changing the rules. One minute they're laughing and being
sweet with you and the next they are being mean and picking
on you for something you have or have not done or said.

You're nothing without me

They might tell you that you're nothing without them:
'You are truly lucky to have me.' It's worth considering
whether you feel lucky to be their significant other –

their bae, their side-chick – as this really means that they perceive you as somehow less than them. The implication is that you are not really good enough for them and they are being kind to you and giving you a chance to prove yourself to them!

How are Mindmixers influenced to behave in this way?

Visual media

We live in a media-driven society. Much of visual media (such as adverts, film, TV and music videos), including social media (Facebook, Instagram, etc.), promotes society's dominant stereotypical norms. It sets up the expectation that males should be big, hench, muscly and behave in a macho way, and that females should be skinny, beautiful, wearing hardly any clothing and moving sensuously or dancing sexily. Most images of people who appear to be 'perfect' are often air brushed. Even when you know that photos are touched up and enhanced, you can still find yourself trying to look like these seemingly flawless people because somehow these images become a benchmark for what looks acceptable. You may think that if you were skinnier or more buff it would please your partner and that they might find you more acceptable and keep them interested in you. The Mindmixer is also led towards comparing you to others. This influence is difficult because this 'ideal' and 'perfect' look is not real so you are unlikely to achieve it even when the Mindmixer tells you that you should.

You can sometimes feel better about yourself when you compare your life to those less fortunate than you. However, comparing yourself or being compared with those who are perceived to be more successful, better looking or more talented can make you feel miserable. There are TV programmes that ask us to comment on others' vocal performance, the way they look and move, their physique and even their beliefs. Similarly, the Mindmixer believes they have the right to compare and contrast those in their path, finding fault and criticising them, particularly their partners. If you don't match up to the ideals portrayed in the media, the Mindmixer can use them in an effort to persuade you that you're inferior so you feel bad about yourself.

A lot of visual media promotes competitiveness and being better than the next person. The media promotes inequality by targeting males and females in different ways, and it also plays a role in promoting the inequality of the sexes. Magazines and YouTube channels aimed at young women focus on how they can better themselves for their partners: how to look better, kiss better, be better in bed and so on. This encourages young women to be overly focused on how they look and perform in terms of being attractive or sexy enough for their partner. With this expectation, the Mindmixer can be drawn into believing there is something lacking if you don't try hard enough in this respect. Unfortunately, a similar amount of energy and airtime isn't on offer to encourage others to see you, appreciate you and accept you for the unique person you are. The same media channels don't promote that young women are more than the sum total of how they look and not enough emphasis or worth is placed on celebrating how diverse, individual, smart, clever, funny, skilled, athletic, capable and kind they are. However, those aimed at young men feature content on sport, outdoor activities, being adventurous and taking risks, as well as having sexualised images of young women or men, depending on persuasion. In the news, males are often depicted as successful for what they have achieved, all of which supports their confidence and self-esteem. However, females often have to endure comments about how they look and their imperfections, rather than the emphasis being on their successes. If the focus of attention is on your imperfections and what's apparently lacking, then this will have a direct impact on your confidence, self-esteem and sense of self. The Mindmixer has the knack to directly reinforce your existing insecurities when they criticise your appearance and the way you look.

In soap operas and dramas there is a lot of sniping, characters putting each other down, family members shouting and being disrespectful to each other, and much use of manipulative and controlling behaviours. They include characters having affairs and picking fights and proving themselves in a variety of different ways. It is this high drama that keeps viewers watching. In addition, some people might also see these behaviours and attitudes in their own families. All of this can leave you with the idea that it is acceptable behaviour; but this isn't the case. No matter how normal these behaviours might seem to you, your family or your partner, it doesn't mean they are acceptable.

The popularity of social media platforms means that you are constantly shown images of your friends and others having fun or being in 'perfect' relationships. There is an unspoken wish to give them 'likes' and seek their approval in return, even when you are only showing them the idealised parts of you – the 'best bits'.

However, we all know that social media can be used destructively. The pastime of poking fun at others, purposely not responding to posts, etc. is common. On a virtual platform it's easy to allow our shadow side to express itself: not having face-to-face contact makes it easier for people to say hurtful things if that is their wish. These behaviours have become normalised in recent years, as if people have a right or entitlement to comment negatively on someone else. Sadly, this phenomenon almost normalises the Mindmixer's behaviour and enables them to embarrass you publicly.

Gender 'norms'

Across the world, every society has behavioural norms – a belief system based on the expectations of how males and females should behave within that society. More often than not, in societies across the world, males are seen as superior to females. This will have a direct impact on the expectations you have about yourself and will affect what you aspire to do in your life no matter what your potential is. This belief system is played out in traditional intimate relationships whereby males tend to take the lead, take control and make the decisions. With control comes a sense of superiority, as well as an inference that having aspirations, taking the lead and making decisions are not what is expected of females. It is worth noting that there is no religion or culture that condones the use of violence or abuse – but there are people, like the Mindmixer, who use their religion or culture to justify their abusive attitudes and behaviour.

Jokes and banter

There are lots of jokes about girls and women being stupid and useless, with girls seen as bimbos, skanks or airheads. For example, blondes are desired but are equally criticised for having 'blonde' moments and seen as airheads. Equally, there are insulting jokes about males who are effeminate, camp, gay, etc. In fact, there are jokes about anyone who differs from the norm. Such jokes are seen as acceptable forms of stereotypical banter, but the context in which they are delivered is crucial. Youth culture promotes banter, throwing short witty sentences to another person that bounce back and forth between the two individuals. Banter can include the use of clever put-downs and witty insults, misunderstandings, zippy wisecracks, flirtation, and puns which are used intentionally in good humour. If there isn't abuse in your relationship, then it can be enjoyed as genuine banter and good humour. However, in the context of an abusive relationship the Mindmixer can use these 'funny' put-downs and say 'It's only a joke', even when it is a direct insult.

Peer pressure

Young men and women tend to value the opinions of their friends, often over and above those of their parents, teachers or adults in general. Often, there is a wish to not stand out from the crowd too much and to identify with the culture of friendship groups. However, this can lead to peer pressure: some people want to look big or popular in front of their friends and to this end can encourage teasing, humiliating and hurting others.

What does The Mindmixer Believe about Themselves and Their Partner?

The Mindmixer believes they are the most important person in their relationship. They are more intent on meeting their own needs and will not consider the impact of their behaviour on others. Essentially, you might say they are self-centred or selfish; they like to get their own way.

Generally speaking, the Mindmixer thinks of their partner as being not as bright or smart as them; basically, their belief is that they are the superior one in the relationship. They believe that you need their help and supervision for everything, or that you are a bit pathetic, useless or lazy. . . a bit of an idiot.

Because of their belief that they are in charge and know better, the Mindmixer expects to be listened to at all times. If you question them they are likely to dismiss what you say as either moaning or nagging. Therefore, they consider themselves entitled to speak to you however they want and to command respect from you at all times. For example, the Mindmixer may have the expectation that you can be moulded to look as they want, and to even change the way you look to suit them. They often have a sense of entitlement that you should do anything they ask of you; if you don't, they will take it as a failing and a sign that you don't love them enough.

As the Mindmixer considers themselves to be so perfect and always right, any objection or reaction from you is taken as an over-reaction or being over-sensitive or demanding. Their view is that you are always the one with the problem! 'It's all your fault.'

WHAT BELIEFS MIGHT YOU SHARE WITH THE MINDMIXER?

You might agree with your partner that you are not as smart or as switched on as they are, and that they are more experienced or know best, especially if they are older than you. You might believe your opinions don't count and that it is easier to go along with what your partner wants.

You may believe that your partner can't help the way they behave because they have mental health issues and think that you have to support them. If you are experiencing poor mental health or have a diagnosis yourself, you might believe you are the one with the problem in the relationship and that it is your fault when things aren't working out or your partner is unhappy with you.

If you menstruate (have periods), you may feel as if you are going mad when you experience hormonal fluctuations, because you can be more emotional, sensitive and irrational at 'that time of the month'. You might even hold the belief that 'there is something wrong with me'.

You may share the belief that you can't make clear decisions and choices or get anything right, and that you should do what your partner tells you because you are too stupid to think for yourself. Consequently, you may believe that you can't be trusted to make difficult decisions and therefore need your partner's help to get things right.

You might believe that males and females are equal or that two people in a relationship should be equal; but you can also hold the conflicting belief that you are inferior in some way or 'not good enough', or that one partner is naturally always more in control than the other and takes the lead. You might believe that someone being controlled by a boy is okay, but someone being controlled by a girl is being 'bitch-whipped'. You may believe it is okay to use the same derogatory language, calling girls slags, whores, hoes or bitches and guys pussies or wimps.

When someone takes control or tells you what to do, you may mistakenly see this as them being bothered enough to do so because they care about you or even love you. You may think they are protecting you and looking out for you.

You may believe the negative things your partner says about you and perhaps share their belief that you are not 'fit' or caring enough and need to change something about yourself. If you feel the need to change the way you look in some way, you can mistakenly conclude that you are not good enough as you are, and that you should be grateful that your partner puts up with you. You see this as being a fault in you rather than a failing in the way your partner treats you.

You may believe that nobody else will ever want you and this relationship is better than not being in a relationship at all. You may tell yourself that your partner is the only person who really cares about you. Interestingly, you never ask yourself: 'If I'm so useless and rubbish, why doesn't my partner end the relationship? Why are they so desperate to be with me if they think they can do so much better?' Neither do you question whether it is the control over you that they enjoy more than their relationship with you. One thing is for sure – there is nothing wrong with you.

How Do you Feel WHeN you aRe TReATeD iN THiS WAy?

There are many ways you can be affected by the Mindmixer, none of which help you to feel good about yourself. Essentially, the challenges of being in a relationship with the Mindmixer can lead to experiencing symptoms of poor mental health such as depression and anxiety.

You may start to feel that 'something must really be wrong with me'. You feel unsure, unable to trust yourself to make a decision in case it is the wrong thing to do. You might overthink things and question yourself all the time, resulting in spiralling thoughts. You see your opinions as useless. Consequently, you feel muddled, as if you have lost the capacity to think straight.

Your confidence is knocked. If you had low confidence before the relationship started, it is easier for the Mindmixer to reduce your confidence to zero. If you had a good level of confidence prior to your relationship, it will definitely be dismantled bit by bit over a period of time. Ultimately, you start to feel useless and that you can't get anything right, especially if the Bully is also at play. This could make you feel on edge much of the time. You feel stupid, naive or foolish and agree with everything your partner says to make your life easier.

You may become confused easily. If your partner says something that undermines you or insults you but in a jokey way or has a smile on their face when they say it, you don't know for sure whether they mean it or not. Are they being nice to me or not? Are they teasing me or being serious? You may believe that the smile means they weren't serious, and it was just a joke and maybe you are being over-sensitive.

You may feel as if you are going mad or crazy, losing a grip on your feelings or losing your mind. This may lead to paranoia or feeling angry and not always understanding quite why.

The Mindmixer gets under your skin and changes the way you see yourself. It is a subtle process and often you aren't aware that it is happening. If someone is being nice to you some of the time, you tend not to consider that they would do anything intentionally to make you feel bad. You don't know what to think anymore; all you notice is your unhappy feelings of being low, tearful, tired and hopeless much of the time. However, you do need to ask yourself: **'Why would someone who says they love me do or say hurtful things to me?'**

How Does it Change the Way You See Yourself?

You might dread logging on to your social media for fear that your partner has posted something about you, put up a photo of yourself that you hate or changed your relationship status for a joke, leading you to feel embarrassed, exposed, humiliated or shamed.

You may start finding fault in the way you look and begin to dislike yourself. You might think that your body is less than perfect or inadequate, that you are ugly inside and out.

You kid yourself that the feeling of being unloved or unlovable will stop if you change how you look to please your partner. When you are consumed by these uncomfortable feelings, you can become so overwhelmed that you believe every part of you is ugly. **However, it is the Mindmixer's abuse that is ugly, not you**.

When you feel so badly about yourself, it can be difficult to know how to manage these strong feelings. There are many ways in which people can be unkind to themselves. Some people want to punish themselves, perhaps by using self-destructive behaviours to help them cope – like drinking too much or getting high all the time. The feelings can be so overwhelming that some people start to hurt themselves (see 'Self-harm' box on page 165).

You might have physical symptoms and start to feel tired all the time, experience a loss of appetite, or need to comfort eat.

Some people develop headaches, tummy upsets and generally feel run down and at a low ebb with no energy or motivation.

A consequence of the impacts listed above is to feel vulnerable. You might want to hide away from everyone and start to pull away from your friends. When you don't have contact with other people, you may even start to think that it is they who don't like you and are avoiding you. You may consider your lack of connection to others as the reason for feeling alone, worthless, sad and unnoticed. It may not occur to you that the way you feel is a direct consequence of being treated so poorly by the Mindmixer. With all these uncomfortable feelings and having isolated yourself, you are left without anyone to reassure you or support you. Carrying all of this alone could escalate to having a panic or anxiety attack (see **Chapter 10**).

LOVED FOR
SIMPLY
BEING
ME

WHO'S LAUGHING NOW?

you keep laughing at me,
Even though you see me crying.
You make me think I'm crazy,
But you're the one who's lying.
You persuade me my friends are fake,
They support me a lot, unlike you who just takes.
My friends are the only people who care
Unlike you who just pushes me to despair.

HOW TO GET HELP

If you recognise any of the feelings identified in this chapter, remember that they are normal responses to the way you are being treated by the Mindmixer. Please know you can recover and feel more like your old self again so be brave, reach out, and connect with a trusted friend, family member or someone you feel you can trust like a teacher, pastoral care or colleague, so that they can support you. It is so important to recognise that you are not alone and there are people who care and can help. Contact one of the following helplines:

- **Childline** for information, advice and support – **tel: 0800 1111** or online chat and email via **www.childline.org.uk**
- See **'Places to Get Help'** (page 277) for a list of websites and helplines where you can get information and advice.

How does The Supportive Partner Behave?

The Supportive Partner doesn't judge you. They accept and love you just the way you are! They encourage and support you to do the things you enjoy, such as sports, hobbies, clubs or studying. They want you to fulfil your goals and dreams because they believe in you. They boost your confidence and value you, your thoughts, ideas and opinions. They are not afraid of you being really good at something that they are not. They recognise you can have different strengths and abilities, all of which are worthy. They help by discussing your ideas with you and supporting your decisions and are patient even when you are unsure.

You laugh and share good humour and banter. The Supportive Partner doesn't laugh *at* you, your thoughts and ideas; instead, they laugh *with* you. You can go out together to places and have fun doing the things you enjoy. As well as having time together you can have time apart to see your friends. You feel able to be honest because you trust one another.

The Supportive Partner talks to you nicely using kind and positive language. They call you by your name and never call you names, except ones that are affectionate and loving because they respect you. The things they say as well as their behaviour will be consistent and won't change from one day to the next, which is reassuring. The Supportive Partner will compliment you and tell you that you are special because they mean it and not because they want something from you in return.

The Supportive Partner believes you are both equal: neither one of you is better or worse than the other, or is entitled to more or less than the other because of your gender. They believe you are smart and can do anything you put your mind to.

The Supportive Partner has lovely qualities that can be seen in the way they treat you and others. They are kind, thoughtful, patient and considerate to family and friends as well as to you. They make everyone feel comfortable around them. They are honest with others, making them trustworthy and reliable. The Supportive Partner always has your back and you face things together as a couple.

THE TAKER

THE TAKER.

Chapter 7
THE TAKER

This chapter focuses on the Taker, one of the five different characters that the Controller adopts. The ultimate aim of the Taker is to be sexual with you without forming a truly healthy relationship and they will stop at nothing to take what they want. The chapter explores why you might want sex, the pressures you are put under to be sexually active, sexual manipulation, the impact of pornography and the dilemma of consent.

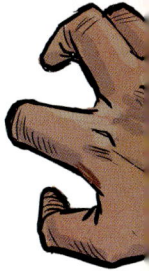

Joe and Lara met at a party. Joe is five years older than Lara. He has made her feel special by saying lots of lovely things to her and spending time with her. Joe is Lara's first love: she hasn't had a relationship with anyone before so it all feels new and exciting. Joe wants Lara to stay over so she constructs a reason to say she is staying with a friend and she goes to stay with Joe instead. They go up to his room and almost immediately Joe pushes Lara on to his bed. There is no kissing and he has one hand over her mouth. Joe is pushing himself against Lara and starts to pull at her jeans. Lara struggles and Joe pins her down. She can barely breathe and is becoming more and more scared and confused by the way Joe is behaving. As he takes his hand from her mouth she screams to him to stop. He slaps her face and tells her she knew what was coming. What did she think she was at his place for? Joe pulls away and doesn't speak. Lara feels as if she has done something wrong and starts to apologise to Joe. He tells her that others he has been with were more sexually mature and he was disappointed in her. He starts watching some porn on his laptop. Lara felt bad and didn't want to risk losing Joe so sat and watched it with him. Joe started saying that if Lara really loved him she would give him a blow job. Lara felt she had no choice because otherwise he would go and find someone else who would.

In this example, Joe has used the characters of the **Charmer** (when he says lots of lovely things to Lara), the **Keeper** (when spending all his time with her), the **Taker** (when pushing himself on Lara and pulling at her jeans, watching porn and telling her to give him a blow job), the **Mindmixer** (when he compares Lara to others and expresses his disappointment in her), and the **Bully** (when he pushes Lara on to his bed, puts his hand over her mouth, pins her down, slaps her face and then sulks).

How Does The Taker Behave Towards You?

The Taker will coerce you to be sexually active or to have sex with them. Having sex is a huge step in a relationship, and it's very normal to feel nervous about it. However, many people go into a sexual relationship for the wrong reasons and the outcome can be destructive or hurtful to themselves. **The only time you should ever have sex is because you really want to.**

Poor reasons for having sex are:

- You've had sex once, so now you believe you have to do it again
- Your partner will leave you for someone who is more willing if you say 'no' to them
- Your partner has been feeling down recently and tells you it will cheer them up
- Other people your age have sex and it seems that it's no big deal to them
- You want to be able to say you have
- You want to impress your partner
- You don't care about yourself
- You are unclear about your values and how you feel about having sex
- You have a duty as a partner to have sex with them
- You want to be or feel rebellious
- You're drunk or too out of your wits to say 'no'
- You like to kiss and touch, so it seems like a logical step
- You're bored
- You're doing it as revenge for something
- You're doing it for money or for a reward
- You believe it will bring you and your partner closer together
- You think it will make you feel loved
- You think it will make you feel like an adult
- You're too shy to say 'no'.

You shouldn't ever feel obliged to have sex for any of the reasons listed above. However, you may find yourself in tricky, uncomfortable or compromising situations due to the context of the situation or relationship you are in, the person you are being sexual with and the extent of your experience. If your partner is equally inexperienced, they may also have confusing ideas and fears about sex and you may be learning about having sex together.

Coercion and manipulation

When you are in a relationship with the Controller and find yourself coerced and controlled, it can feel like you don't have a choice in how things happen. Your entire experience of sex is made worse by the Taker because you very likely can't be honest about how you feel and are afraid to say 'no' when you don't want to be sexual.

The Taker can use a variety of statements to coerce you into having sex. Their words are designed to make you feel responsible for their sexual pleasure rather than engaging in a mutually pleasurable experience. The Taker will disregard what you want and play on your feelings of love for them or your desire to please them, or they may emotionally blackmail you into giving in.

In the spirit of having fun, the Taker might encourage you to drink or take drugs so that you become more relaxed. Once you are under the influence of alcohol or drugs – either drunk or high – your resistance is lowered, and you are easier to manipulate and coerce.

'You'd have sex with me if you were sober, so **why not now?**'

'You're so much sexier **when** you have had a couple of drinks.'

The Taker might take advantage of your love for them to abuse you by romancing you and being extra nice, telling you that you are the best partner they have ever had and that you will always be theirs. They wouldn't hesitate to tell you that they love you simply so they can have sex with you – they will tell you whatever they think you need to hear. In the heat of the moment you may confuse their words and coercive behaviour for love.

'**It's fine because** I love you.'
'Sex will make us **stronger** as a couple.'
'I'd have sex with you **whenever** you wanted it.'

The Taker might treat you to drinks, or pay for something else when you go out together, or buy you gifts, which may lead you to feel a bit like you owe them something. If they buy you sexy underwear, you might feel under pressure to wear it for them even when you don't feel comfortable doing so.

'I bought you that present the other day, and **this** is how you say thank you to me.'

The Taker will pester you and tell you that you have to do 'it' and if you loved them, you would. They will convince you that their friends are getting 'it' and it is normal to want sex all the time. This infers you aren't a 'normal' partner if you don't want sex all the time too. They might suggest that you're frigid if you don't want 'it', which implies there is something wrong with you. They may threaten to cheat on you or to leave you if you don't have sex with them.

'If you don't do it with me then **you don't love me**.'

'**I'll leave you** unless you have sex with me. I can find someone else who really wants me.'

Saying 'No'

Sex should be fun and you both want to enjoy it. If you don't feel comfortable to have sex, whether it is for the first time or the hundredth, you have an absolute right to say 'no'. And if, for instance, you wisely choose not to share your social media passwords and your partner insists, you have a right to say 'no'.

'No' is a complete sentence and that is all the explanation that should be required; however, in an abusive relationship 'no' may not be heard and respected. How it is said can make a difference. Believe one hundred per cent that when you say 'no' you mean 'no' and it is not up for negotiation.

Bullying tactics

The Taker can be very pushy! If you aren't immediately taken in by all the 'lovely' things they say to you, your experience can become rather more uncomfortable when they start shouting at you or making threats to coerce you and ensure you give in to them.

The Taker will try looking angry with you in your presence so that you become scared of them. This doesn't necessarily mean they are actually angry but it is the beginning of threatening behaviour towards you. It is a guaranteed way to instil fear and communicate that they have the potential to be aggressive towards you. They may even take the behaviours of the Bully further and threaten to hurt you and be violent if you don't give them what they want.

If a person – either your partner or anyone else – overwhelms you by using physical strength and/or force to do things sexually that you don't want to do, it is sexual assault and/or rape.

RAPE AND SEXUAL ASSAULT

Rape is the act of forcing someone to have sex when he/she is unwilling, has not consented and is against their wishes. This includes penetration by a male of either the vagina, anus or mouth with a penis. If penetration occurs, without consent, either by a male or female, with the use of any other body part, other than the penis – for example, fingers, tongue or by using an object – this would be defined as 'assault by penetration'. The act of sexual or indecent assault can be a physical, psychological or emotional violation in the form of a sexual act, inflicted on someone without their consent. For example, being forced to watch others or participate in the sexual act, being groped, grabbed or touched sexually.

Many people still believe that rape is something that happens at the hands of a stranger. In fact, the majority of people who have been raped knew the rapist; for instance, the rapist was the person they were in a relationship with, their ex-partner, a friend, colleague or other family member. Rape can also happen in marriage when one person doesn't have the capacity or freedom to say 'no'.

Rape can be reported at the time of the assault or years later. If you report the rape within seven days of it happening, your clothing can be used as forensic evidence. You can seek help and information from a Sexual Assault Referral Centre (SARC) where people who are expertly trained are available to talk with and you will be safe. They will store your forensic evidence and will not pressurise you into reporting to the police until you feel ready to.

If you report to the police, they may bring charges against the person who raped or sexually assaulted you. This can result in them having a prison sentence, fine or a community order and being put on the Sex Offenders Register.

The Taker might be very sexual towards you, groping you and grabbing your breasts or 'bits' when you are alone or in public places in front of others. They might push you into doing things with their friends as if they can 'share' you. The Taker might force their hands into your underwear or try to 'dry hump' you.

The Taker might try to demonstrate that you 'belong' to them by 'marking' you with what are commonly known as 'slag tags', 'hickies' or 'love-bites'. These are actual physical wounds and bruises that can hurt.

Confused

Why does he do it? Does he not care?
He just takes me anyway, whilst I simply stare.
It is supposed to be loving, that's not how it feels
He says in a few days your body will heal.

But it doesn't matter at least not to him-
He constantly tells me, I'm just not like Kim
she was my best friend, what did she do?
she gave him a blow job, and his mates too!!

What can I do? I feel trapped inside
Responding to his needs, but ignoring mine.
He says this is normal, get used to it babe,
If you want to be with me, you'd better behave

Cos I can replace you whenever I like
It doesn't feel normal, it doesn't feel right.
Morbid thoughts visit me in the middle of the night.
I really thought he was Mr Right.

Will I be happy? I guess not with him-
I think I'll reject him so he can go back to Kim.
Then I can escape the hell that I'm in
And build my own future without him.

PORNOGRAPHY

Pornography today is more prevalent and easier to access online than ever before and it is changing the way people perceive sex within a relationship. Porn can be too easily viewed by children and young people long before they reach sexual maturity. Much of the porn available is hardcore and those viewing it will be bombarded with, in particular, images of women and young girls being utterly dehumanised in the sexual act. The sexual acts performed are totally removed from the context of any caring relationship. There is no storyline and no conversation or communication taking place between the people involved and this has changed many people's expectations of what sex in a relationship should be like. This is especially true for young people, many of whom will have viewed porn before having had sex in a relationship.

Today, many people's early experiences of sexual intimacy are not intimate and loving at all because they are either required or are expected to perform a 'sexual' act, or somehow the expectation of this has been instilled in them.

Pushing the boundaries

The Taker might make you watch porn or play video games in which women are humiliated or raped. You might then be encouraged to do the things you have watched even if you feel uncomfortable about doing so. They may call you abusive names whilst you are doing this.

The Taker might persuade you that if you loved them, you would have oral sex and further, let them come in your face or swallow their come. Many young people are unaware that being pushed, forced or coerced into doing oral sex when you don't want to is an act of rape (see 'Rape and sexual assault' box on page 144).

The Taker will very likely ask you to text sexual pics of yourself (tit-pics, pussy-pics or dick-pics) to them, saying that they are missing you and want to see your body. They might then threaten to share the images on social media for all your friends and family to see. The sharing of such images – **sexting** – is a criminal offence, and yet it is on the increase. If you are under 18 years old and you send, upload or forward indecent (sexual) images or videos to your friends or partner, even if they are photos of yourself, this would be breaking the law. It is also a criminal offence for your partner to share one of these images or videos with others.

The Taker may even want to take things further and film you. They might ask you to touch yourself while they film you. This may appear to be part of your sexual relationship and something personal between you both; however, any pictures/photos or film footage of you can potentially be used to blackmail you. Worse still, it may be posted on social media for all your friends and family to see. This is commonly known as 'revenge porn'.

You can report nude/sexualised images to prevent them being uploaded – see **Childline** in the 'How to get help' box on page 176.

REVENGE PORN

Revenge porn, also known as 'non-consensual pornography' or 'cyber-rape', is when a partner/ex-partner posts sexual images or footage of their partner online or in messaging apps in order to degrade and humiliate them. It typically occurs when the victim chooses to end the relationship. **However, it is not really 'porn' because you were in a sexual relationship with the partner when the image or video was taken.** The term 'revenge porn' is a bit misleading as it implies that you might willingly engage in porn, which is not the case because, as far as you are aware, any such filming or photography was within the context of your personal relationship. The language of 'revenge porn' also suggests your partner is 'getting you back' for something you have done wrong; however, ending a relationship because you don't want to be with that person anymore is not wrong — you have the right to end a relationship.

The term 'non-consensual pornography' aims to make clear that **consent** wasn't given; however, it is misleading because at no point was the victim partner consenting to **any form of 'pornography'**. Perhaps the term 'non-consensual exposure' might be a better way of labelling this humiliating action.

WHAT DO THE TAKER'S PASSIVE AGGRESSIVE BEHAVIOURS LOOK LIKE?

It is easy to recognise the passive aggressive Taker because they are very good at withdrawing affection from you: they will stop looking at you, smiling at you, making eye contact with you, cuddling you and even though they seem to be wanting sex they will withhold sex. If they have been flirty and attentive and you have felt sexually desired and wanted at other times in the relationship, and then suddenly they show no interest in you, it can lead you to think you've done something bad or wrong.

They might resist getting intimate with you at all and in response you may feel responsible to do anything you can to ease the tension and give them what they want. If you were to let your partner know that you would like sex with them by coming on to them, they may use the opportunity to push you away or put you down. Such rejection can be very difficult when you are trying to be loving with your partner.

Alternatively, your partner might come on to you and appear to be really into having sex with you but prematurely ejaculate (come very quickly) and then ignore your needs, leaving you feeling rejected and frustrated.

How is the Taker influenced to behave in this way?

A lot of what the Taker believes has been influenced by the way physical appearances and sexuality are portrayed in the media. Girls and young women, in particular, are encouraged to be hyper-sexualised and to 'pornify' themselves. Wherever you look — be it magazines, posters, advertising campaigns, TV dramas, game shows or music videos — sexy women promote and sell more or less everything, implying women are a commodity. Across the media it is not unusual to see women posing in sexualised or scant clothing, in full make-up, botoxed and/or with breast enlargements and a facial expression that says 'fuck me'. Women are presented in this way as though it is the ultimate norm, suggesting that the sexualised aspect of a woman is her only real asset or value.

During our teen years we develop our individual sense of identity, and it is important to feel visible as well as respected and acceptable to our peers. If you don't have this sexual value or '**fuckability**' look about you, you might worry that you will become invisible to, and of no interest to, your peers and others. You may also believe that conforming to a certain sexual body image is the way to attract a partner and keep them, and that this is ultimately how you will find love. The messages are conveyed to both genders and reinforce the expectations of how we should look and behave in our intimate relationships.

Society places pressure on how we should perform sexually: young women to being 'up for it', proving they are fun-loving and 'up for a good time' but to not be 'sexually demanding', while young men are pressured into demonstrating how sexually accomplished they are, including being dominant in bed. Young men are given the 'toxic masculinity' message (see page 86) that they should be preoccupied with sex all the time, that they 'need' sex, that this is what 'real' men want, that they are entitled to get what they want and can use aggression to get it. It is implied that this is a normal part of what guys do. All of these messages and expectations – some of which enter our subconscious without us even realising it – can very easily lead you to believe that you'll only find a level of acceptability in relationships if you are sexually active. If you don't choose to respond in this way or aren't feeling 'up for it', then you can be deceived that you are underperforming. The Taker will exploit this pressure by pestering and shaming others for not wanting to conform to these demands.

The game of pursuit and onscreen consent

The game of pursuit is present at the onset of many relationships. In the heterosexual context, young men are fed the message that they must pursue and chase the girl to demonstrate their interest, whilst at the same time young women are conditioned to believe that they should play their part in the game by being 'hard to get' and resist the attention of the person who is pursuing them so as not to appear too 'easy'. This dynamic is known as 'token resistance'.

Dramas and films often use the 'token resistance' dynamic by depicting scenes and storylines where a woman consistently says 'no' either to the offer of a relationship, or to sex, but then after persistent pursuit and bombardment (by the Charmer) gives in and says 'yes' to sex and appears to enjoy it. This scenario carries the message that if someone keeps pestering and pursuing a person they are interested in, who initially wasn't interested in having a relationship or sex with them, their refusal or saying 'no' actually means, 'ignore what I say, keep trying and you can have me'. These films and dramas are made for our entertainment and the characters are fictitious, and the situations aren't real. However, these portrayals of how to establish a relationship and get sex influences the Taker to believe that it is okay to push you to see them and have sex with them, even when you say 'no'. It reinforces the typical notion that when a woman says 'no' it is not what she means. It would be wonderful to see a drama in which guys hear the word 'no' and are cool with that! How empowering it would be to see characters building a relationship rather than playing out the 'token resistance' dynamic, which simply reinforces the myth that the person being pursued didn't know their own mind!

CONSENT

Consent means giving your permission for something to happen. If you believe you are in a loving relationship, you may think you have to have sex to demonstrate that you love your partner. However, if you are going along with it but don't really want to or are doing it because you think you should, or have to, it is not consent. You 'consent' to sex only if you agree by choice and have the freedom and capacity to make that choice.

If someone makes you feel bad or hurts you physically in the process of sexual contact, it is abusive behaviour, and this is not acceptable. Having sex should be a brand-new decision each time it is a possibility and each time you have sex you should consciously consent to it.

You can give your consent for one sexual activity but don't have to for another; for example, you might consent to have vaginal intercourse but not anal sex, and you might only agree to penetration with conditions, such as wearing a condom. You can withdraw your consent at any time during sexual activity. If a person has sex with you without gaining your consent it is rape.

Dating apps

There are dating apps aimed at young people that emulate those designed for adults, which enable you to hook up with people you have never met with the likely expectation that you will have sex. Meeting someone on an app that identifies where you are can be very dangerous. Be aware that these apps are also used by unscrupulous people for grooming, sexual coercion and exploitation, and sexual assault. They also reinforce the Taker's belief that sex is something that should be available to them at all times and on their terms.

Gender roles

In many cultures, gender roles are perceived as being fixed, with one person always being more dominant in the relationship, or in the family, as well as in the bedroom. In some cultures, there is no expectation for the sexual fulfilment of females, with the emphasis on sexual fulfilment for males. In this context, it would be considered immodest for a female to have sexual desire. Based on these cultural beliefs, the male Taker in a heterosexual relationship considers only their own sexual pleasure as being important. Across all cultures, females who demonstrate sexual desire, try to initiate sex or simply have a high sex drive are often viewed negatively and are perceived to be 'up for grabs'. However, having sexual desire is healthy and normal and does not mean you are a 'slag'; neither does it mean that you are 'up' for being harassed, groped or sexually assaulted.

Pornography

The Taker is also influenced by the prevalence of pornography and 'soft porn', which includes music videos that highly sexualise women and are viewed by men, women and children of all ages. Porn online showing abusive sex is especially harmful to the younger audience. Young people who watch this type of porn can become overwhelmed by the images that cause them to feel sexually aroused and excited, whilst at the same time feeling a sense of shame and self-loathing because they are being excited by something they know to be abusive and harmful.

If a young person doesn't know what sex is meant to look like prior to watching porn, they may mistakenly think of porn as 'normal' sex. They may not recognise that pornography is a form of abuse. Therefore, the Taker might not realise that the way they treat you is sexually abusive. And because they are aroused by watching porn, and believe that what they have seen onscreen is normal, they may think that these porn scenarios are what needs to happen if you want to enjoy yourself sexually.

The context of a relationship is rarely seen in porn: you never see people having fun, going on dates, laughing, talking to or showing consideration for one another. Porn sex doesn't look anything like the sex you have in a healthy relationship: it isn't the same as 'making love' because there are no emotions associated to it. Porn confusingly depicts sex as 'fucking' (whether vaginal, anal or oral), which looks non-consensual and sometimes involves the rape of one person by several people. If the Taker has watched a lot of porn, this is how they will likely treat sex. If they have been heavily influenced by porn they may even want to share you with their friends, which is a form of sexual exploitation.

Here are some things that porn suggests about sex that are NOT true:

✗ Women and men both always want it when the subject is broached

✗ No matter what happens, both parties always enjoy it

✗ There is little or no discussion before having sex to work out what the other enjoys

✗ The people involved like being forced into doing something

✗ Sex is rough and fast all the time, and everyone uses kinks to orgasm

✗ All penises and breasts are huge, and anything less isn't good enough

✗ Women are objects men have sex with

✗ There must be an imbalance of power for it to be enjoyable

✗ Women will enjoy whatever is done to them

✗ Men must be more dominant during sex.

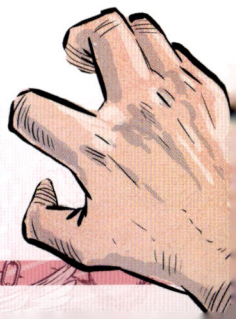

You Say You Love Me

You Say You Love Me
Why do I feel so dirty?
Why do I burn in shame?
I try to keep you happy,
yet you say I am to blame.

Apparently, I am not normal,
I am frigid through and through.
Because I hate the things you do to me,
And make me do to you.

You must think that I am stupid,
I know you creep downstairs,
In the night, out of sight,
To watch porn film players.

You say that you love me,
And beautiful is my body,
yet you treat me like a piece of meat,
And your care of me is shoddy.

You say I don't respond to you,
That I am too still and dry,
If you treated me like a human,
I wouldn't need to cry.

You leave me with bruises,
Both inside of me and out.
This really cannot be normal,
I am truly filled with doubt.

You give me painful infections.
With your 'life choice' of not to wash.
As I lie here in your fluids,
The urge to vomit I have to quash.

Yes, you have taught me a lot,
How to pleasure a man with sex,
But the biggest thing you taught me is,
That your pleasure shows no respect.

I now know you didn't love me,
Just abused me for your kicks,
I now know that I am normal,
And that healthy sex is bliss.

WHAT DOES THE TAKER BELIEVE ABOUT THEMSELVES AND THEIR PARTNER?

The Taker will hold particular beliefs about the gender roles and rights of males and females and how you are supposed to behave in your sexual relationships.

The Taker may believe that they have a big sexual appetite and need regular sex, holding an absolute belief that you belong to them and are there only to please them, and that they have the right to have sex with you when and how they want. If your partner believes that your role is to sexually relieve them and meet their needs, they will infer that you should always be 'up for it' and you don't have the right to say 'no'; and if you loved them, then you would gladly have sex with them! The Taker wants his partner to always look sexy and be a bit of a cock-tease; but at the same time, he considers that she is 'asking for it' when dressed like a slag, ho or slut.

The Taker doesn't understand the word 'no' and appears to see this response as you teasing and playing hard to get – that 'no' really means 'yes', and this is reinforced if you have said 'yes' to sex previously. Further, the Taker may reason that if you would just 'give it to them', they wouldn't have to take it.

The Taker may also believe that contraception is not their responsibility and they can have unprotected sex if they want it. In their eyes, contraception is therefore solely their partner's concern.

WHAT BELIEFS MIGHT YOU SHARE WITH THE TAKER?

You may believe that sex is natural and can be a bonding experience – and of course in the right circumstances it can be. You might believe that your partner has a bigger sexual appetite than you and needs regular sex, and because you are in a relationship with them it is your responsibility to always be 'up for it' and please them. You may consider that having sex is important because it shows you love them and are serious about them and your relationship.

If your partner is particularly nice to you when they want sex and only tells you they love you when they are getting sex, you might believe you need to have sex to show them you love them. This may even lead you to think this is the only way to demonstrate love and the only way to get a cuddle and feel wanted.

You might believe that sex is the way to 'kiss and make up' after there has been an incident or a disagreement between you.

If your partner is older than you and appears to be more experienced and behaves as if they know what they are doing, they might say things like 'my ex did it' and so – whether or not it's true – you may believe you should do it too. You may believe that it is normal to experiment when you have a partner no matter what your age. If your peers are having sex, it may seem that it is acceptable even at a younger age. Perhaps you have been encouraged to believe it is just fun and doesn't hurt anyone.

If you are shown porn, you might think you should act more like a porn star to keep your partner's attention. You may believe this even if you don't feel comfortable doing it! Eventually you may think that sex and porn are the same thing.

You may believe that sex is what you do when you are with someone, that it is just what you are expected to do. And if you don't want to have sex and say so, and it still happens, you may not realise it is rape. Also, you may think that it isn't rape if it's 'just' a blow job you are being required to give. Further, you may believe you have to swallow your partner's come because it shows your partner you love them.

You may believe sex isn't good with a condom because your partner tells you this and refuses to wear one. This may also lead you to believe you are responsible for using contraception and for protecting against sexually transmitted infections (STIs) or diseases (STDs).

Alternatively, you might believe that the only thing anyone wants you for is sex, so you see it as your only means of power: a way of getting some affection, attention, love or a boost to your self-esteem.

How might you feel when you are treated in this way?

Sadly, there are plenty of uncomfortable and upsetting feelings you can have when forced to do things of a sexual nature that you didn't want to or felt unable to prevent. And to make matters worse, none of these feelings are easy to express.

Confused

If your partner has coerced you into having sex you can feel confused because the coercion is happening in the context of your relationship, whether this appears to be a full-on romantic, loving relationship or is more casual, motivated by sex. You may struggle to accept that the person you love or have strong feelings for could abuse their power and push you into something you don't want to do or aren't ready for. Such an experience is disconcerting because it is a betrayal of the trust you have placed in them. As a relatively young and inexperienced person, your sense of self as a sexual being is quite fragile, making you hugely vulnerable at this time, particularly if you have feelings for the person you are with. In some circumstances, this could put you at further risk of your partner sexually exploiting you along with other people.

The coercion and pressure to have sex can be subtle and lead you to believe that you have consented. You may have consented to sex but may *not* have consented to doing things of a sexual nature that made you feel uncomfortable. You can feel stupid, pathetic and duped, and consequently you might tell yourself that you should have somehow known better. You may then blame yourself for making the wrong choice; however, it can be deceptively easy for someone to find themselves in this situation. The reality is that it is never your fault if you are sexually coerced and assaulted. It is quite normal for anyone who experiences sexual coercion and abuse to feel humiliated, degraded, dirty, unclean and too shamed to tell anyone what has happened to them.

You can be left feeling cheap and worthless, to the extent that maybe you don't even think you're worth the care you so very much need after being abused in this way.

THE DIFFERENCE BETWEEN FEELING ASHAMED AND SHAME

Feeling ashamed means you are embarrassed or feel guilty because of your own actions. It indicates that you understand right from wrong behaviour and it can often prove to be a useful experience. If you do something wrong or say something unkind to another person you might be told off and feel guilty for doing something 'bad'. Feeling ashamed can support you to make a different choice about how you behave in the future.

Shame is a painful feeling of humiliation or distress caused by the abuser's shameful behaviour towards you. It can result in self-judgement and self-hatred for what has happened to you as if it were your fault. It is as if you take on the belief that this bad thing happened to you because you are bad in some way. It is likely you will experience a loss of self-respect, and a perceived lack of honour causing low self-esteem (see page 232).

SELF-HARM

People can experience many uncomfortable feelings and not know how to alleviate them. For example, you may be angry at the person who coerced you to do something you didn't want to and because you didn't feel safe enough at the time to express that anger you hold on to it. Sometimes the anger and contempt are turned inwards and when this happens you may blame yourself for not stopping it. Such distorted thinking can lead to **self-harming — the act of hurting oneself on purpose, often to cope with unhappy or painful feelings**. It is likely caused by not knowing how to put into words the way you are feeling or how to ask for help. Wrongly, some people believe that self-harming is a vain and attention-seeking behaviour: when someone is suffering in this way it can be more helpful to view it as 'attention *needing*'.

Some of the most common forms of self-harming are: cutting, scratching, burning, pinching, excessive scrubbing, marking your body, hitting or biting yourself, or using substances like alcohol or drugs to excess. Substances are used to numb painful feelings so you can't recall clearly what happened or connect with the experience easily, and this is an attempt to forget that the painful experience(s) ever took place. Eating disorders can develop due to the increased feeling of anxiety, shame, anger or self-loathing — perhaps of the person's body image. Controlling food intake by either eating too much (comfort eating), or too little can give the person a sense that they have control over something, even though it is harmful to the body and a dangerous thing to do.

At some stage in your relationship you may have shared naked pics of yourself with your partner or they may have even filmed you having sex. If your partner tries to blackmail you by threatening to post these photos on social media for everyone to see, you may feel you have no choice but to go along with whatever is being demanded because you are frightened this may actually happen (see 'Revenge porn' box on page 149). In this situation, you might feel completely degraded, humiliated and exposed. The shame you feel may lead you to isolate yourself and, fearful of the response of anyone who may have seen the pics or footage, it is likely that you avoid your friends and family and stop going out.

Similarly, if you have been threatened that something bad will happen if you speak to someone about what you are experiencing or feeling, you may withdraw from seeing people. You can feel hugely exposed either because you have been subjected to the sharing of an image of yourself or because you feel so raw and vulnerable. You might imagine that other people will sense what has happened to you and consequently take on the blame for it and avoid those close to you. Once you start to isolate yourself, you feel more alone and unacceptable, and you can start to believe that nobody cares about you. You may even convince yourself that other people are rejecting you, when in reality you are pulling away from contact with others. If you cut yourself off from others and don't connect with people who care about you, you can start to feel invisible and believe there is nobody there for you. When you are unseen and alone, it is easy to believe you are invisible: nobody sees you or hears how you feel or what you have been through. If you don't feel seen or heard, you will start to feel worthless and believe others will hate you too.

You may believe that if you don't go along with the sexual demands of your partner – and any future partner – that they will reject you. The feeling of rejection can be so uncomfortable that you might hold on to relationships longer than is good for you, just to protect yourself from the pain of rejection and being left alone. Sometimes, however, the cost of avoiding rejection is just too high.

Feeling powerless

You may feel trapped by your partner, finding yourself in a situation where you have not consented, you don't want to do any of the things you are being pushed or coerced into doing and you know that you are not safe to say 'no'. There is a defensive process that your body and mind go through to protect you when you are feeling powerless and being hurt that can be described as the Five Fs – Friend, Fight, Flight, Freeze and Flop.

FIVE Fs –

FRIEND, FIGHT, FLIGHT, FREEZE AND FLOP

Initially you might try **Friend**, being super 'friendly' – trying to talk to the person who is attacking you to distract them or say nice things to them in an attempt to make them stop what they are doing. If this doesn't work the next stage of defence is **Fight**. You might try saying 'no', resisting or fighting the person hurting you. This may be difficult if they are using aggressive and violent behaviour and are stronger than you. When you can't fight back, the brain starts to release hormones to activate and energise your body into **Flight**. This is an instinctive response, not one you have time to think about. At this stage you will look for ways to hide or escape the situation to make yourself safe. If there is no opportunity to get away, your brain will automatically put you into **Freeze**. Your brain shuts down your capacity to think and feel to protect you from further injury and emotional pain. Freeze is often described as feeling nothing, numb, frozen or paralysed. **Flop** is the final stage and happens when freeze is not enough because you are still in a situation of significant threat. Flop is when the mind and body literally go 'offline', becoming soft and floppy: you become submissive, appearing to 'give in' to whatever is happening to you with no protest, because this is the safest thing you can do in that moment to survive.

The Five Fs response is not something you consciously decide to do – you can't control it. Therefore, when you don't say anything your silence does not mean 'yes'. However, because you don't say 'no', it is too easy to tell yourself that you went along with it, so perhaps it really is your fault. If you think for one moment it is your fault, you will automatically take the blame, and more specifically you will carry the shame. Your abuser will reinforce this conclusion.

FRIEND · FIGHT

FLIGHT · FREEZE · FLOP

Long-term effects on your mental health

If you have been in situations where you have been sexually coerced, and felt pressurised and threatened, you can become jumpy, shaky, nervous, anxious, constantly afraid of it happening again or fearful of what will happen if you try to refuse, and this is known as being **hyper-vigilant**. In experiencing any of the impacts of sexual coercion, it would not be surprising if you developed **trauma-related symptoms** like flashbacks (memories of your trauma), sensory triggers (often connected with the five senses of sight, smell, sound, touch and taste – typically a sharp noise such as a bang or a slamming door, a particular song or music genre, the tone of someone's voice, shouting, use of a specific word, a place or room or a particular smell), panic attacks, anxiety (see **Chapter 10**) or dissociation (feeling as if you are there but not there, like being behind a glass screen and being able to see everything, but not feeling connected to it).

You can go into a kind of 'empty space' in which you experience yourself as numb, lifeless or dead, known as being **hypo-vigilant**. It is normal to feel this way when you have been through a sexual and/or physical assault or series of assaults. The brain automatically shuts down the feeling part of yourself (the 'freeze' response) so that you don't keep re-living the feelings associated with the assaults. It is not a sign of madness and you are not going crazy, even though it may feel like it. When your situation changes and you feel safe enough, you will be in a better position to deal with the feelings held in your body.

However, if your situation doesn't improve it is possible that you may experience **depression** – feeling numb and irritable for the much of the time, a constant lowness that feels impossible to escape or persistent sadness for a long period of time, losing interest in things that once gave you joy, lacking in energy, and experiencing trouble sleeping and concentrating. Some people with depression may find it difficult to get out of bed in the morning because they wonder what the point is, and others may look healthy to the outside world but inside they feel utterly defeated by unhappiness.

Over time when you feel helpless, powerless and too weak to stop what is happening to you, these feelings gradually undermine your ability to escape. It can also make you feel like giving up on everything and, potentially, suicidal thoughts may enter your mind as the only way out of the trap you are in. Suicidal thoughts, as the term suggests, occur when you repeatedly think about killing yourself, and consider acting on these thoughts. Generally, **suicidal thoughts** are not actually about wanting to die, but relate more to wanting the pain or the difficult situation you are in to end. Even though suicidal thoughts seem like logical thoughts, they are a sign that your mind is not in a good place at this time. Suicidal thoughts can be caused or exacerbated by sleep deprivation, hormonal imbalances (e.g. just before a period, when hormones affect your mood) or enhanced by drugs and alcohol which you may be using as a coping mechanism. It is hard to have faith that your feelings and situation won't remain the same forever, but this is more often the case. Your feelings ebb and flow – they are changeable – and even the worst of feelings will lessen eventually even if it seems difficult to believe at the time.

If you have experienced any form of poor mental health, it is essential that you find someone to talk to – but **not** your controlling partner. Choose a trusted friend, family member, GP or a reliable person at school, college or work, or even a therapist to talk to in person. Alternatively, contact one of the helplines listed in the 'How to get help' box on page 176 to talk on the phone or via a chatline. Without a doubt, sharing it with someone will ease the burden of what you are carrying. There is an old saying: 'A problem shared is a problem halved'. It really does feel better to talk to someone rather than not.

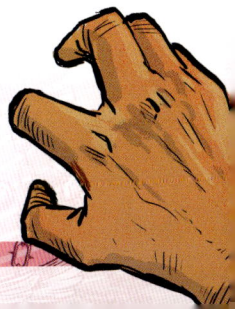

The effect on your body

You may be very fearful of getting pregnant. If your partner hasn't used contraception, or allowed you to, you have all the pressure and burden of getting the morning-after pill or making lifelong choices about having a baby, etc.

You may have been given a sexually transmitted infection or disease (STI/STD), many of which can have lasting impacts on your physical health and the health of your babies in the future. You would also have to warn all future partners about the STI/STD, which can further add to your experience of humiliation and shame. As a result, you may feel scared of future intimacy or sexual activity.

You might start to develop a poor relationship with your body, perhaps feeling ashamed because it drew attention to you and brought you such horrible experiences. You may begin to dress in ways which cover you up so that you draw the least attention to yourself. You might feel the need to 'wash away' what happened to you and scrub yourself frequently. It is as though the abusive experience gets under your skin and you try as hard as you can to cleanse yourself of that feeling. Victims/survivors of sexual assaults and sexual abuse can also develop eating disorders (see 'Self-harm' box on page 165).

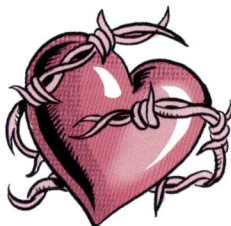

How Does The Loving Partner Behave?

The Loving Partner wouldn't do anything you were uncomfortable with and would not pressure you into having sex and would be listening to whether you want it or not. They understand that when you say 'no' you mean 'no' and it is not up for negotiation. 'No' is a complete sentence and that is all the explanation they would need. They are considerate and accept that sex will happen when you are both ready and you will move at a pace that feels comfortable for you both. If you don't feel comfortable to have sex, whether it is for the first time or the hundredth, you have an absolute right to say 'no' and you will be heard, regarded and respected.

Sex for the Loving Partner is not a deal breaker! They would be supportive and ensure that the environment is right and that you have somewhere 'safe' to have sex, i.e. a place where you can discuss what you feel happy to do sexually and feel safe to experiment. The Loving Partner cares that you are both relaxed, even if it is your first sexual experience or indeed theirs. Sex should be fun and you both want to enjoy it. They treat your body with care and are bothered as much about your pleasure as their own. They want to know what works for you.

The Loving Partner can be romantic and is generally comfortable showing affection, holding your hand and putting their arm around you. They enjoy cuddles and kisses with you and hugs without expecting that it will lead on to sex. They might organise dates with you where you can do things together and be close.

They will check out with you how you're feeling so that you can be honest and open with each other. If things are going too fast or something doesn't feel right, the Loving Partner will stop – particularly if you ask them to. They communicate with you, so you can make these decisions together. If you didn't want to have sex they wouldn't sulk.

The Loving Partner respects that your sex life is private, and they wouldn't think of telling others about what you do. You would discuss and take responsibility for contraception together. They would support your decisions around the contraceptive pill vs other forms of protection.

The Loving Partner will respect and appreciate your beliefs and values and your culture and religion, if you have one. They appreciate that these aspects contribute to making you the person you are, and they would love you for that.

HOW TO GET HELP

If when reading this book, you recognise that you have been sexually coerced or assaulted please know that there are things you can do to help yourself. Try talking to a trusted friend, family member or someone you feel you can trust like a teacher, pastoral care or colleague, so that they can support you. It is important that you don't hold on to the experience alone. Alternatively you can:

- Contact **Childline** for information, advice and support – **tel: 0800 1111** or online chat and email via **www.childline.org.uk** If you are under 18 you can use the website to securely report nude/sexualised images to prevent them being uploaded: search for the 'Report Remove' tool and you will find clear instructions. When reporting in this way, it makes no difference whether you shared the image willingly or were coerced or groomed.

- Call **999** to report the assault to the police. You are entitled to ask specifically for a female or male police officer if you will be more comfortable talking to them.

- Contact your local **SARC** (Sexual Assault Referral Centre). SARC services are designed specifically to help people who have experienced rape, sexual assault and sexual abuse. There is a SARC or Rape Crisis in every county and the following websites can help you find the one nearest to you:

NHS – Find your nearest SARC via **www.nhs.uk**

Rape Crisis – **tel: 0808 802 9999** or chat live via **rapecrisis.org.uk**

The Survivors Trust – Free helpline: **08088 010818**
www.thesurvivorstrust.org

- Go to your local doctor's surgery as soon as possible so you can receive any necessary medical help and support. Your **GP** will be able to give you STI/STD tests and the emergency contraceptive pill (morning-after pill), which you must take within three days of the assault to avoid pregnancy. To be sure, it is wise to also take a pregnancy test after three weeks.
- Find a **counselling service** to help support you emotionally. Whilst it is important to talk about what has happened, you do not need to go through your experience in detail. After what can be a very traumatic event, it is vital to reach out, enabling you to recover and minimise any harmful, long-term impact of the experience. Look for a local service online and ensure that the counsellors are registered with a professional body of practitioners such as:

  BACP – British Association for Counselling and Psychotherapy

  UKAHPP – UK Association of Humanistic Psychology Practitioners

  UKCP – UK Council for Psychotherapy

  BPS – British Psychological Society

  COSCA – Counselling and Psychological in Scotland.

- See **'Places to Get Help'** (page 277) for a list of websites and helplines where you can get information and advice.

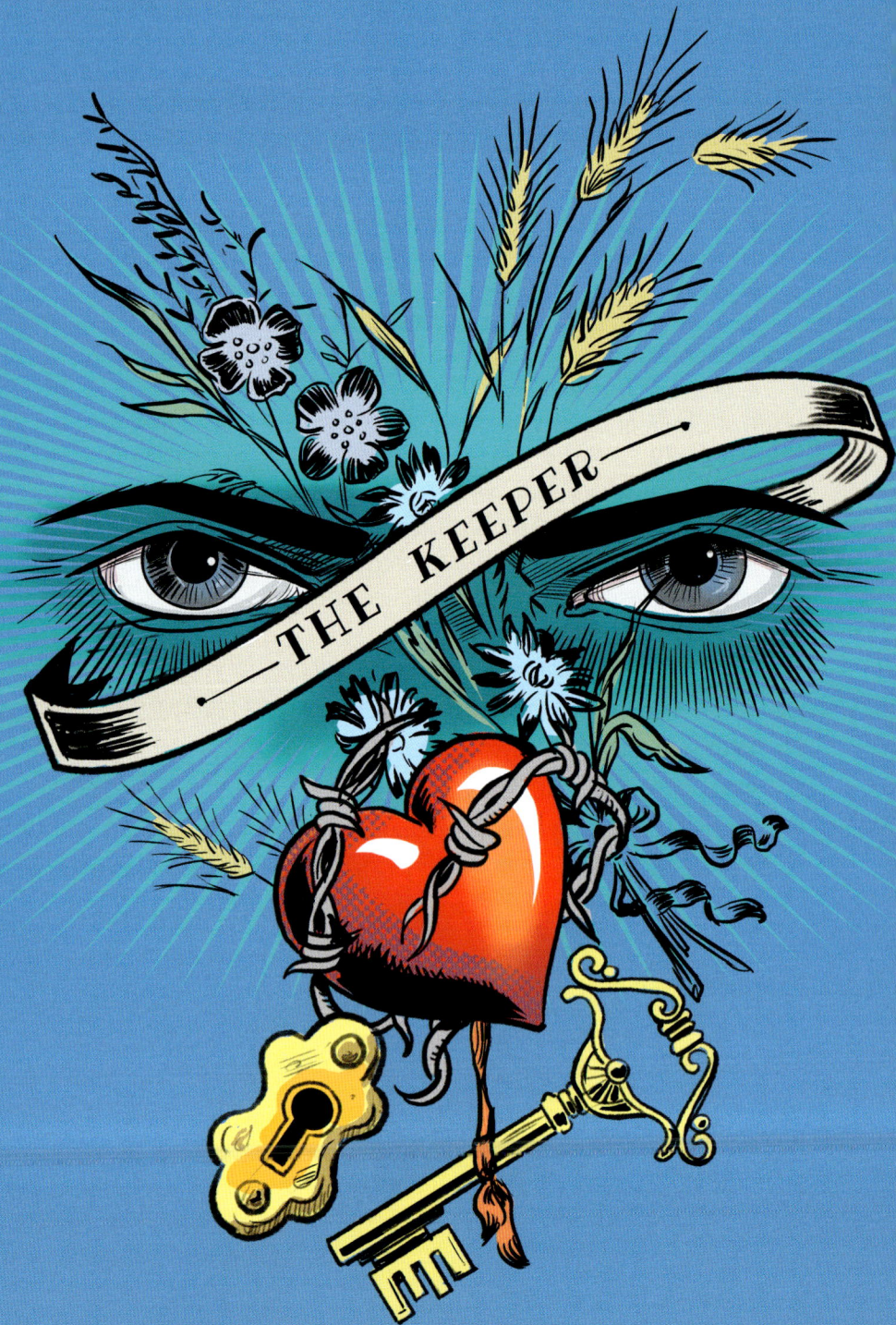
THE KEEPER

Chapter 8
THE KEEPER

This chapter explores the Keeper, one of the five different characters that the Controller adopts. The Keeper's sole aim is to isolate you from your friends and family, making you dependent on them. Once isolated and on your own, you become easier for them to control. They want you to be with them all the time and will stop at nothing to achieve this.

Stevie and Charlie have known of each other for a while but have only been together for a few weeks. Stevie is a keen footballer and plays with a club and that is how they first met. Charlie seemingly accepts that Stevie has football and study commitments that leave little time for them to see each other, but Charlie starts dissing the club and making comments about Stevie being flirtatious with other players. Stevie reads this as jealousy but doesn't take it seriously. Charlie persuades Stevie to miss practice a couple of times so they can see each other for date nights. Charlie is also constantly messaging Stevie, which is hugely distracting. If Stevie doesn't acknowledge the messages, Charlie becomes moody, sulks and makes nasty comments to Stevie that are both personal and about the football team.

Stevie's parents notice things aren't right and share their concern about Charlie's behaviour not being as supportive as it should be. When Stevie tells Charlie this, Charlie gets into a mood and starts throwing things around the room, including Stevie's phone which gets smashed and broken. Stevie feels scared and worries about going anywhere because of the persistent messaging and unkind comments, and ends up thinking: 'It just isn't worth the hassle'.

This example includes the characters of the **Keeper** (when Charlie accuses Stevie of flirting with the other players, encourages Stevie to miss practice and persistently sends messages), the **Mindmixer** (when Charlie makes nasty comments about Stevie), and the **Bully** (when Charlie gets moody and throws things, smashing Stevie's phone).

How Does The Keeper Behave Towards You?

The Keeper will try to separate you from your friends and do everything they can to turn you against them. It is a clever idea because if you don't have friends, you become more dependent on them for company, acceptance and approval. To achieve this, they might use devious tactics such as flirting with your friends and passing it off as banter or they may say that when you weren't around, your friend made a pass at them. In response you would probably have this out with your friend and question them as to why they have done such a thing to you. Your friend would naturally be upset or annoyed that you would entertain such an outrageous thought and as a consequence you might fall out with them. It won't look like your abusive partner stopped you from seeing your friend because they didn't directly tell you not to see them. Typically, you won't see your partner as a bad person; rather, it will be your friend who looks like the bad one.

The Keeper could also achieve this by telling you that they heard your friend(s) saying something mean about you when it isn't true. Why would you doubt your partner? After all, they are supposed to like you, care about you and love you. You might put it down to your friends being jealous that you are in a relationship, etc. In this situation, you will try to rationalise or make sense of what you are told rather than doubt the sincerity or truth of whatever lie you have been fed.

The Keeper may also encourage you to skip school or college or miss lessons to be with them, suggesting that you call in

sick or simply bunk off lessons. You may tell your friends that you are sick and start telling fibs. If your friends find out they might start to think you can't be trusted or feel miffed that you don't trust them enough to tell them what you are doing. This can cause rifts and dampen your friendships.

Staying close to you

If you are at the same school or college as your partner, they may demand you to see them during every break. They may wait outside your classroom after each lesson and want to walk you to your next lesson. This allows you no freedom to do anything by yourself like walk with your friends or talk freely to others. It could be worse still if your partner is in the same lessons as you because they will be watching everything you do and everyone you speak to.

Whether they are at the same school or college as you or not, they may insist on walking you there and back again from home or vetting who else does. Without discussion, they may even move to be with you once you leave college and go on to university!

The Keeper will ensure they become your main focus. The easiest way for your partner to get your attention is to tell you they love you so much they can't be without you. Everyone wants to hear they are loved and special, and you are more likely to accommodate the partner who tells you this. They might say they will be miserable without you, which is especially coercive if they have also presented themselves with any kind of 'mental health' issue and are low or depressed.

'I'm feeling really down at the moment.'
'I feel a bit lost when you aren't around.'
'My anxiety is really bad right now.'

The Keeper might tell you they had trust issues with a previous partner and will insist on going everywhere with you, therefore you can't do anything alone or with family or friends. If they aren't interested in going everywhere with you, they might try to put you off doing the things you want to do like going to clubs or spending time on hobbies.

Family rifts

The Keeper can turn you against your parents. They may text you constantly while you are at home, so you are preoccupied with them rather than being with your family. Your parents might worry about this and question you or ask you to leave the phone outside your bedroom at night. However, because your partner is intent on controlling what you do, they might try to persuade you that your parents are being unreasonable and don't care about you, and that they don't 'get' you. This can be enough to drive a wedge between you and your parents. When you are in a relationship you feel more grown up and it is easy for you to believe comments like:

'They treat you like a child.'
'Your parents don't want you to grow up.'
'Your parents don't understand you like I do.'

Once you are intent on spending as much time as possible with your partner, despite your parents expressing their concern and telling you that this isn't okay, your partner might suggest that you live with them and their family. At this point it will seem like a great way of resolving the difficult situation at home and you are unaware that your partner has cleverly constructed the situation for them to be more in control. It also gives the impression of you being acceptable as a couple in a more adult relationship in your partner's home.

However, things could get much worse from here. Your partner may start telling you who you can and can't be friends with and who you are allowed to talk to when you are out. They might also tell you that you can't go out, which leaves you at home when they go out with their friends. Sometimes they might leave you at home with their family! Over time, you may fall out with or lose contact with your own friends just as you have fallen out with your family and, consequently, will feel more alone than ever. In an extreme situation, you may experience being locked in the home or unable to leave because you don't have keys to get back in.

Getting you pregnant

If your partner has refused to take responsibility for or won't allow the use of contraception, in time you are likely to become pregnant. Being pregnant makes you even more dependent on the Keeper because you might now be very isolated from your friends and family and believe you have no one else to support you. If you have experienced physical assault before the pregnancy, it is likely that the abuse will get worse **during** pregnancy, statistically increasing by as much as 33 per cent. If you have never experienced any physical or sexual assaults before pregnancy, it is more likely to happen for the first time during pregnancy.

What do the Keeper's passive aggressive behaviours look like?

Stopping you from going out without them

The passive aggressive Keeper might prevent you from going out by starting an argument with you just before you are due to set off to visit your friends or family. The argument is designed to hold you up, make you late, or make you feel so rotten that you decide you don't want to go anymore. If they were meant to be coming out with you, they might use tactics such as not getting ready in time or trying to hold you up by saying they aren't feeling well; they are concerned about something; they have doubts about one or all of the people you are meeting; they are cynical and negative about your plans, and so on. In reality, though, they just don't like doing something they don't want to do and have no intention of putting themselves out for you.

Another clever way to prevent you from going out is to tell you that you will be unsafe if you went out alone, or were out late at night, so much so that you might be fearful of going out alone or at all. They might then offer to give you a lift, so you will feel a bit safer and then at the last minute claim that the car is making a funny noise and shouldn't be driven.

Another trick of the passive aggressive Keeper is to abandon you when you are out with them by just hiding, disappearing or creating a scene and walking off. This could be in the middle of nowhere or in the centre of town late at night, leaving you feeling scared and vulnerable. Alternatively, you might be babysitting with them, and they storm out after creating an argument so you can't leave the children or the house. Even if they apologise to you afterwards, you may still not feel safe to go out with your Keeper again after that. This is another cunning way to stop you wanting to go out, cutting you off from others.

Your partner might be really lovely to you when you are out with your friends and appear to be loving, friendly and easy going, but behave entirely different when you are on your own. The Keeper will have made clear to you that you have certain rules to abide by regarding what you can and can't do when you are out.

'When you go out you **can't talk to anyone you don't know**.'
'You **can't have more than two drinks**.'

They may even suggest that these rules are necessary because you behave like a flirt or a bit of a 'slag' when you have a couple of drinks and you can't be trusted when you are out. The Keeper might try to reason with you that they are trying to be helpful and look out for you. The Keeper will watch you constantly when you are out, and this can look as if they are attentive to you and it would be hard for others to imagine your partner has imposed such rules on you.

Putting up a pretence

The passive aggressive Keeper may give you the impression that they care about you by saying they love you and that you should pursue your goals and so on but, in reality, they don't support you with your hobbies, interests, clubs or studies – things you may have been pursuing for a long time before you met them. They find ways to distract or keep you from engaging with them.

The Keeper might appear to encourage you to see your friends, but then accuse you of flirting with other people or, worse still, cheating on them. They then get angry, saying they can't trust you, and behave resentfully towards you.

The Keeper might take your schoolbooks or school bag, so you don't have what you need to go to your lessons. Or you might have your school bag but your bus pass, travel card or bank cards have been taken.

Using your phone to control you

Much of the abuse received online from a partner or ex-partner is part of a pattern of abuse you also experience offline. Your partner might try messaging your friends pretending to be you and say things that aren't true – perhaps that you will meet them somewhere at a certain time or that you have heard something about them which isn't very nice. A friend might believe you or go to meet you, and – of course – you don't turn up.

The Keeper might text or message you all the time. This might seem attentive and a sign that they care about you and are interested in you; however, they will expect you to message them frequently too and will appear to get angry if you don't reply to their messages immediately. They might ask for pics of where you are or who you are with or ask you to live-stream from the places you go.

Your partner may have provided you with the gift of a brand-new phone, laptop or another piece of technology, which at face value seems generous of them. However, they may have enabled the GPS tracker that shows where you might be at any particular time or uploaded apps that require your location to be included. In extreme situations, they may even have the apps installed on your phone, tablet or laptop linked to their own devices. This tracking of your whereabouts at all times is called **digital stalking**: the Keeper doesn't need to keep turning up where you are and following you because they have the additional advantage of doing this remotely using technology. They may also view your online history and might check to see what sites you have been on, what you might want to buy, where you might want to go and where you might have been seeking advice and information.

As part of their digital stalking, the Keeper will likely check up on your social media by browsing your timeline, updates, conversations, photos/videos, profiles and friends. It can also include checking what you have written on other people's timelines or retweeted. This means they would be able to see any contact or conversation you have had with friends or family.

If they have access to your account(s), the Keeper can delete your friends and followers. Unless your friends are really close to you, they will likely take offence and unfriend you in response.

In the spirit of sharing and being honest and open with each other, your partner may demand passwords to your devices and social media. If you don't want to or say 'no', you will be told you must have something to hide and perhaps be accused of cheating or not loving them enough. Once they know your passwords, they can post things as if they are you. Worse, they could change the passwords, so you struggle to open your own apps! In some cases, the changing of passwords doesn't just include social media, but your online bank account and potentially taking your money or controlling how much money you can access from your own accounts.

How is The Keeper influenced to behave in this way?

Gender roles and expectations

Messages about gender roles and expectations are fed to society through adverts, soap operas, dramas and films. They demonstrate gender-typical roles either within the family unit, the home or the workplace and in the hobbies and interests that people enjoy. For example, female characters in traditional dramas are seen at home, caring for children or family members despite the fact that they may also be working themselves; their worlds revolve around the family

unit and/or home that they live in. Meanwhile, men are depicted as coming and going from the home more regularly, for work or for travel, and not as being tied to or restricted in the home or by the family unit. Adverts show, for example, men and children dumping muddy clothes and sports kit on the floor and women picking them up and putting it all in the washing machine as if only women know how to do the washing; or present information to women on which cleaning products they should buy; or show families around the dinner table eating food that the mother in the advert has cooked. These females are always smiling and appear to be radiantly happy, giving you, the viewer, the message that being at home and doing these jobs will lead a woman towards a sense of satisfaction and fulfilment. The implication is that the role of a woman/mother is to make everyone else happy. These images reinforce the expectation – and the Keeper's belief – that women belong in the home.

Trust and ownership

Trust and ownership are huge issues for the Keeper. In soap operas, dramas and films, females are often characterised as being deceptive, sneaky and manipulative and who will stop at nothing to get what they want. In this onscreen world, it would be considered suspicious if such a character wanted to go out, see friends, work and have a life independent of their partner. Meanwhile, a male character will blindly and naively trust their partner, who then has an affair, proving that females simply can't be trusted. The portrayal of these gender roles build up and reinforce stereotypical behaviours, even though the programmes and films are made

purely for our entertainment. When one's expectation of stereotypical roles and behaviours are challenged and people don't behave as expected in their gender-typical way, it can lead to a climate of mistrust.

In our society, there is a strong message that once you are in a relationship you can be treated as if you belong to the person you are in the relationship with, which has been established over centuries. For instance, in most cultures and faith systems a father 'gives his daughter away' at her wedding, as if she is his possession to give away and not a person of free will in her own right. Also in the transaction of marriage, women make vows to love, honour and obey. Though society has changed somewhat over the last few decades, the notion that we belong to one another is still as strong today whatever the blend of relationship. You may have experienced a version of this ownership yourself; for example, being dictated to about where you can go, who you can see, and on what terms. Quite possibly this has been done as if there is a set of rules about what you can and can't do in a relationship. The term 'obey' alone indicates that we should tell our partner what they want to know when they want to know. The notion persists that when you are in a relationship you should be honest and open about everything and have no secrets. It is absolutely safe to be this way if you are in an established loving and respectful relationship, but not at all helpful to anyone in a coercive and controlling relationship.

191

Social media

Social media enables everyone to be seen and to promote what they are doing. A young person's posts generally describe to their followers what they are up to and where they are doing it, as well as tagging their friends in photos, etc. By making people's lives so public and information about them available it gives the impression that others have a right to be told, kept in the loop and updated. However, the Keeper will take this to an extreme level.

Instilling fear

Society is instilling fear by sending out messages about how hazardous it is to be out on your own. You are led to believe that it is dangerous to be out at night, in the dark and that you need protecting from these dangers. To some extent it is implied that you are stupid to be out alone and therefore, if something bad happens to you, it is your own fault. Through childhood you rely on your mum, dad or carer to keep you as safe as possible by taking you to and from the places you need to be. In your teens, if you go out without them, you are encouraged to call or message regularly to say you have arrived somewhere or are ready to be picked up. You are told that it is much safer to be out in a group with others, inferring that if you aren't you have something to be fearful about. The Keeper can use the fear that has been suggested to you to look as if they are protecting you by walking you or driving you to places to keep you safe. This is very noble and generous in a loving and respectful relationship, but not so in a controlling one. From the Keeper's point of view, they can keep tabs on everything their partner is doing when on the surface they appear to care about your safety.

WHAT DOES THE KEEPER BELIEVE ABOUT THEMSELVES AND THEIR PARTNER?

The Keeper believes that you would be up to something they wouldn't approve of if you went out on your own. The Keeper doesn't believe you can be trusted and so would be suspicious that you'll do things behind their back and not as you have been told. If you are on your own or not with them, you will certainly be less easy to control. The Keeper suspects that if you want to go out, it can only be to meet other people; and if you do meet other people, you might go with someone else. The Keeper doesn't really trust anyone and may truly believe that you are not safe if you go out on your own.

The Keeper is so focused on you that they believe your priority is them because you are in a romantic relationship together. They see your friends and family as being not as important and a threat to their control of you. They think they have a right to control you as if you are their property and you should be at home. The Keeper fears that if you had the chance to see friends, you might tell them what is happening to you or share how you feel and if they are exposed in this way, your friends or family might try to persuade you to leave them.

WHAT BELIEFS MIGHT YOU SHARE WITH THE KEEPER?

You might believe you belong to each other. This sense of belonging and feeling special to your partner may be something you like because you assume that they must care about you. Perhaps you don't want to think about yourself not being with someone because you might believe you are nothing if you are not in a relationship.

If you grew up in a family where your mother did everything for her partner, you may believe that you should do the same to keep your relationships. If your mother was a 'stay-at-home mum' who cared for the family and the home, you may consider this to be completely normal. If your mother was 'kept' by her partner, you may grow up believing women need looking after.

You might have got drunk a couple of times and been a bit rowdy or were told by your partner that you behaved in this way. This could lead you to believe that you can't trust yourself when you are out and that you need your partner to keep a check on you, telling you what you can and can't drink. You may believe they are just looking out for you.

Consider what you think about your friends who are in relationships when they do things without their partner. You might assume that your friends don't want to be in relationships if they don't spend all their time together with their partner. You might think that it's not normal to do things separately and that you should do everything together.

You might believe that if people do things separately it gives them the opportunity to meet other people, and this may not feel comfortable. You may wonder that your friends might not love their partners or be serious about them.

How Do you Feel WHeN you ARe TReATeD iN THiS WAy?

At first, you may feel fully committed to being with your partner all of the time even if it means you neglect your friends and family. It feels new and exciting, and you make every effort to plan everything around seeing your partner. However, as time passes and you start to see less of your friends, it can begin to feel awkward or more difficult to message them or make plans to see them. This is made worse still if your partner has created difficulties or conflicts between you and your friends. When you see less of your friends, you start to feel isolated and disconnected from them and ultimately, you may feel left behind by them or that you don't have a friend to turn to.

Your friends may try telling you that they are concerned or worried about you, that they don't like some aspects of your partner's behaviour towards you. Typically, though, you will not want to hear this and will not want to even consider that you have got your partner 'wrong'. In response, either you don't listen or you dismiss what they say and carry on. Your friends may get frustrated with you, which can also be difficult to cope with. It may appear that they turn their back on you;

however, they have tried to support you but you haven't listened to them. When they walk away from you or you from them, it can **seem completely unconnected** to the coercive behaviour and control of your partner.

Sadly, when being coerced and abused by the Keeper and believing your friends don't want to see you anymore, you become more reliant on your partner than ever before. This reliance and sense of loneliness as well as the ongoing abuse will lead you to feel trapped in the situation. When you are no longer having contact from friends and those usually close to you, this loss of connection can lead you to feel like you have lost yourself a bit – lost your own identity and you don't know who you are anymore, although you may try to kid yourself that you are all right on your own. This can be very confusing as you no longer have the confidence to rely on yourself to know how to handle or resolve a situation.

Sometimes it can feel as if you have been pulled apart and broken so you no longer recognise yourself or how you respond to your experience with your controlling and coercive partner. This growing disconnect can make you feel very vulnerable and cut off. You can feel as if you don't have any control over your own life.

HOW TO GET HELP

If you recognise that you have been isolated by your partner, try taking a leap of faith and contact a trusted friend, family member or someone you feel you can trust like a teacher, pastoral care or colleague, so that they can support you. It is important to realise that you are not alone and there are people who care and can help. Alternatively you can:

- Contact **Childline** for information, advice and support – **tel: 0800 1111** or online chat and email via **www.childline.org.uk**
- Contact **Brook** for advice on sexual health, pregnancy and wellbeing – **www.brook.org.uk**
- Use **hand signalling** if you are online with a friend or family member but are unable to speak to them directly. Hold your hand up to the camera with your thumb tucked into your palm, and then fold your fingers down trapping your thumb in your fingers to indicate that you are trapped.
- See **'Places to Get Help'** (page 277) for a list of websites and helplines where you can get information and advice.

The Mask

I wear a mask on most days to hide how it is I really feel.
I wake up in the morning with a heavy heart, a pressure
building in my chest.
I place a mask upon my face to make me look my best.
A work of art I have created. Will it stand the test?

Worthless, useless and empty I'm desperate
to leave it in the past
This reflection I see of myself in the mirror,
how long will it last?

My mask is smiling whilst all I want to do is cry,
my body and my mind are tired.
My mask is hiding so much more than people are aware.
Always so conflicted on whether I should share.
The way I really feel inside, who would even care?

I'm a kind of tired sleep can't fix.
I'm stuck between trying to live my life and
trying to run from it.
I get told life's too short for loathing any
storms beneath your skin
But how do I show myself, when it is easier to let them win.

TRUST
AND BE
TRUSTED

How Does The Freedom Partner Behave?

The Freedom Partner is the opposite of the Keeper. They are comfortable with not being in your company all the time, enabling you to enjoy time with other friends and family.

The Freedom Partner has lots of great qualities: they are thoughtful, considerate, kind, helpful, supportive and encouraging. If there is a difficulty, they will work it through with you.

The Freedom Partner encourages you to see your friends and family and doesn't complain when you want to do things socially with them. They are relaxed with your family and don't try to sneak off with you all the time. They are comfortable enough that they don't need to prove themselves in any way and can happily 'go with the flow', joining in with things you may all do together.

The Freedom Partner trusts you with other people. This means that they are more likely to encourage you to keep up your hobbies and clubs because they don't feel threatened by the friends or the people you meet doing them. They show an interest in what you are doing rather than asking tons of questions about who you see and what gender they are. They believe you when you talk to them about the people in your social network, whether this contact is in-person or via social media. They respect your privacy on social media and don't interfere with it or ask you to share your passwords and log-in details.

The Freedom Partner believes in your right to independence. You are freely able to make choices about when you go out and where you go. They may only voice a concern if they have one that is related to your safety. They are not threatened by your independence but enjoy that you are independent.

The Freedom Partner believes everyone should be treated fairly and that you are both equal, whatever the gender dynamic of your relationship. They don't hold huge expectations of how you should behave because of your gender. They love and appreciate you just as you are.

The Freedom Partner wants you to do well. They enjoy you as a person and want to support you in all you wish to do. They may help you with your homework or studies and won't mind if you help them. They enable you to get to school, college or work and will encourage you to believe in yourself. They will tell you that you are 'good enough' and clever enough to achieve your goals and dreams.

Chapter 9
HOW TO SPOT THE CONTROLLER

In order to keep yourself as safe as possible in your new relationships, there are behaviours you can look out for in the first few days/weeks that might help you to make a more informed decision about what you do next: (a) continue with the relationship knowing there are obvious signs of abusive or coercive behaviour; or (b) walk away from the person, saving yourself from not only dangerous behaviours, but also the heartache, pain and misery that are inevitably experienced in any controlling and coercive relationship.

Now that you have examined the five characters of the Controller and their different behaviours and beliefs (**Chapters 4** to **8**), you may have learned something more about your past partners or even your current partner. Just as important – but perhaps a bit uncomfortable – you have hopefully learned something more about yourself.

Someone who genuinely cares about and respects you would not use any of the pushy and overwhelming behaviours of either the **Charmer**, the **Bully**, the **Mindmixer**, the **Taker** or the **Keeper**.

KNOW YOURSELF

The most important relationship you have in your life is the one with yourself. If you know the qualities you hold – whether they are good, bad, naughty, cheeky or endearing – you are more able to accept who you are as a person. And with this self-knowledge you can be one step ahead of the possibility that someone will take advantage of you. Knowing yourself brings confidence and insight, enabling you to be more aware of what is going on around you or happening to you. You can develop a more helpful self-belief not tied to the views and opinions of others – free to be the way you want to be and not be influenced by someone who wants to control you in some way. Learning about yourself is a life-long project.

The Charmer

Everyone is charming in the first flush of romance in the early days. It is okay to want someone to be super lovely towards you, spoiling you and declaring their love for you – this is the dream. In the first few days/weeks it can be difficult to work out whether some of the behaviours of the Charmer will lead to abusive behaviour, but below are some that many people experience:

- **Compliments you**
- **Is super nice to you**
- **Says things like 'I've never felt this way before' and 'I don't deserve you'**
- **Wants everyone to know that you're dating**
- **Tells you they love you**
- **Tells you that you're special**
- **Wants you to be their 'baby mother'**
- **Wants to 'marry' you**
- **Brings you flowers or gifts**
- **Treats you to something**
- **Has a 'sob story' (poor me)**
- **Behaves in an overfamiliar way towards you, like they have known you for ages**
- **Is super charming to your family or friends when they meet them.**

The Bully

Much of the time, the Bully is quite easy to identify. Below are some clear and obvious behaviours that many people experience in the first few days/weeks:

- **Sulking**
- **Pushing**
- **Dirty looks**
- **Ignores you**
- **Speaks in a loud, dominant voice**
- **Swears at you**
- **Physically pins you down**
- **Plays rough and calls it 'banter'**
- **Gets in your personal space**
- **Starts fights with other people**
- **Smashes or breaks something in front of you**
- **Damages walls or property in their home**
- **Pretends to strangle you**
- **Assaults you then blames you**
- **Drives too fast.**

The Mindmixer

The Mindmixer is less obvious than the Bully and can be harder to identify in the first few days/weeks, but below are some key signs:

- **Gives you a nickname**
- **Calls you names**
- **Taunts you**
- **Teases you about personal issues, like the way you look or what you say**
- **Fires questions at you**
- **Laughs at you**
- **Compares you to others**
- **Pays you backhanded compliments**
- **Says something unkind and smiles or laughs as they say it**
- **Puts down things you say**
- **Makes you feel childish**
- **Says you are too sensitive**
- **Accuses you of being too emotional**
- **Wants to know your secrets**
- **Mocks your values and beliefs.**

THE TAKER

By recognising that the Loving Partner wouldn't be thinking about engaging in sexual activity — which is a big deal — in the first few days of seeing you, the Taker can be more easily identified. The following are obvious and key indicators of the Taker to look out for in the first few days/weeks:

- **Constant sexual innuendos**
- **Telling you their ex did it all the time**
- **Sexting dick pics**
- **Pestering you to sext a tit-pic, pussy pic or dick pic**
- **Shaming the pic you sent them**
- **Encouraging you to get drunk, stoned or wasted**
- **Asking you to watch porn**
- **Wanting to touch you constantly**
- **Groping you in public or in front of friends**
- **Flirting with others**
- **Making sexist jokes**
- **Pushing you to have oral sex.**

The Keeper

As with the Charmer, it can be difficult to believe that some of the Keeper's behaviours are considered abusive. You might prefer to think that the following behaviours are a sign that your partner is really into you and cares about you. The key here is **context**. Some of these behaviours may seem completely normal in the first few days/weeks. You may also want to spend all your time with this new partner and getting to know them can feel intense.

- **Constant texting**
- **Wants you all to themselves**
- **Wants you to spend all your time with them**
- **Encourages you to skip school, college or work**
- **Wants to come everywhere with you**
- **Status change on social media to 'in a relationship' and tags you in**
- **Wants to know your passwords**
- **Wants to set up joint social media accounts**
- **Wants you to come off social media**
- **Tells you they don't like something about your friends**
- **Questions what you are doing or who you are with**
- **Tells you that your parents don't 'get' you or they treat you like a child.**

What you say about them

You can find yourself saying things about your partner which also give you clues about the nature of your relationship.

Initially, many of the statements on page 211 might sound protective, caring and as if your partner really likes you; however, when the statements are read with close attention a **pattern of control** can be observed. Each of the statements demonstrates controlling behaviour **dressed up** as support, being protective and wanting the best for you. If you have had previous relationships, you will have heard yourself say the same or similar things about your own ex or current partners, so **allow this awareness to act as a warning sign** next time.

Always remember who the Partner is and how they behave (see **Chapter 2**) – there is no better starting point. The Accepting Partner (see page 77), the Caring Partner (see page 99), the Supportive Partner (see page 134), the Loving Partner (see page 174) and the Freedom Partner (see page 200) will all behave well towards you in the first few days/weeks and will continue to do so throughout your relationship. You will instinctively feel able to trust that they will stay this way and will support you with your best interests at heart.

'My partner loves me **SO MUCH** they want to be with me all of the time.'

'My partner says I should be honest with them about EVERYTHING.'

'My partner says they will tell everyone I'm frigid if I don't have sex with them.'

'My partner sends me LOADS of text messages ALL the time.'

'MY PARTNER SAYS I'D LOOK GREAT IF I DID MY HAIR DIFFERENTLY.'

'My partner turned up at college as **a surprise** to walk me home.'

'MY PARTNER ALWAYS WANTS TO KNOW WHAT I'M DOING.'

'My partner doesn't like me talking to other people, even my friends.'

'My partner says I don't love them if I don't want to have sex.'

'My partner gets **really jealous** if someone else looks at me.'

'MY PARTNER WANTS ME TO SHARE MY PASSWORDS.'

'MY PARTNER HAS A NICKNAME FOR ME AND USES IT ALL THE TIME.'

'My partner doesn't want me to meet their friends in case they fancy me.'

'My partner wants me to send pics of EVERYONE I am with, so they don't miss out!'

'My partner says their last partner had sex with them ALL THE TIME.'

'MY PARTNER SAYS I UPSET THEM WHEN I DID SOMETHING ALONE WITH MY FRIENDS.'

'My partner doesn't talk much about their ex, just says I am the one.'

'My partner says they REALLY fancy me and can't stop touching me all the time.'

'My partner has got me tipsy a few times and says it will **relax me**.'

'MY PARTNER ENCOURAGED ME TO SKIP COLLEGE SO WE COULD GO OUT FOR THE DAY.'

Part 2:

TAKE B
CONTE

Take Back Control

Now that you have read about the five characters of the Controller and their different types of behaviour, you may have identified with some of the uncomfortable impacts of being abused in your relationship. Part 2 includes information and tools that will support you to manage and process the difficult and painful feelings you have as a result of your experience. It also shows how the Controller changes their behaviour when they suspect that you are thinking of leaving them and offers help to escape the trap you find yourself in and end your relationship safely.

Chapter 10

DEALING WITH FEELINGS OF OVERWHELM

Being overwhelmed by our feelings can be so difficult to bear and to manage. We can really believe that we are going mad and losing control of our mind even though overwhelm is a temporary experience. This chapter looks at panic attacks and anxiety and offers some simple techniques to enable you to manage these feelings. It also includes some strategies to help reduce the experience of anxiety.

Some of the things you experience in an abusive or coercive relationship will have a direct impact on how you feel and experience yourself and the world around you. Any of the following can result in you having panic attacks and anxiety:

- **Experiencing fear and trauma either as a child or as a teenager in your relationships, also known as developmental trauma**

- **Experiencing ongoing stress and worry due to conflict in personal relationships**

- **Being an anxious person generally**

- **Having symptoms of depression or other possible mental health issues**

- **Using drugs or alcohol**

- **Living with fear of being attacked because of your social differences (e.g. gender, sexuality, religion, ethnicity).**

PANIC ATTACKS AND ANXIETY

It can be difficult to know whether what you are experiencing is a panic attack or anxiety because they can be experienced similarly. Generally, a panic attack appears to come from nowhere, is severe, disruptive, short-lived and a more intensely felt experience. Anxiety has milder symptoms that build gradually and can last from a few minutes to several hours and sometimes they can continue for days. Anxiety can range from mild to severe and is always there in the background of everyday life. Sometimes anxiety can lead to panic attacks.

WHAT IS A PANIC ATTACK?

Panic attacks can come on very quickly and without warning and they can be very frightening to experience. The onset of a panic attack may not be related to anything happening in that moment. If you have had one you will recognise some of these symptoms:

- Feeling weak, faint or dizzy
- Tingling or numbness in your hands and fingers
- Feeling hot and sweaty or cold and shivery
- Strong pain or tightness across your chest
- Difficulty catching your breath, breathlessness or feeling unable to breathe
- Nausea or feeling sick
- Ringing in the ears
- A choking sensation
- Feeling as if you have no control over your body
- Trembling or shaking uncontrollably
- A feeling of having hollow legs or wobbly 'jelly-like' legs that are going to give way
- Feeling disconnected from yourself or the people or place around you.

Having a panic attack is such an overwhelming experience: some people describe it as feeling like they have completely lost control, and others think they are having a heart attack and fear they are going to die.

> The average length of a panic attack is about **10 minutes.** Generally, they will be at their worst or peak within 10 minutes, but they can last between five and 20 minutes.

217

What is anxiety?

Anxiety does not occur so suddenly as a panic attack but it intensifies over a period of time, is often associated with extreme fear and worry, and can be accompanied by a wide variety of symptoms. Some of these symptoms are experienced as feelings and thoughts and others are experienced physically in the 'fight or flight' response (see pages 168 and 169). The most common symptoms are listed below.

Feelings

- A feeling that something really bad or frightening is going to happen

- Feeling like you are losing control or going crazy

- Having a heightened sense of being in danger and needing to stay on guard, known as being hyper-vigilant

- An overwhelming sense of gloom, hopelessness and maybe distress

- Feeling strange or weird in yourself

- Confusion and difficulty thinking clearly, like your mind has gone blank

- Being irrational – unable to see things as they are, a bit like being detached from reality

- Difficulty concentrating

- Trapped by the fear in your mind

- Feeling you need to escape

- Feeling like things aren't real, but like a dream or outside of your body, known as dissociation.

Physical symptoms

- Dizzy, lightheaded or unsteady, as if you might fall over
- Feeling you might pass out or faint
- Pounding or racing heart
- Breathlessness or feeling you can't catch your breath
- Tightness in the throat or a choking sensation, like something is stuck in your throat
- Dry mouth
- Hot or cold sweats
- Feeling a knot in the stomach, tight stomach
- Abdominal pain or an upset tummy
- Needing the toilet urgently
- Butterflies in the stomach
- Feeling sick or actually vomiting
- Feeling like crying
- Headaches
- Numbness
- Pins and needles
- Tingling or shaking uncontrollably
- Problems sleeping, resting or feeling relaxed and calm
- Tense muscles or twitching.

The experience of anxiety varies: sometimes there are very few symptoms and then at a different time you might experience many of the symptoms listed.

Either way, anxiety is a normal reaction to danger: it is the body's automatic 'fight or flight' response that is triggered when you feel scared, under pressure or threat of danger or harm over a period of time. When anxiety is experienced over time, it may have an impact on the way you live your life; for instance, you might avoid certain people or places for fear that they might trigger a panic attack or intensify feelings of anxiety.

Everybody is different and each person has a different idea about fear and pain and how they judge what is happening to them. Generally, your experience of the symptoms will depend on how frightened you are and how you react to what you are frightened about. People also have different levels of awareness about what they experience, with some people more tuned-in to their bodies and able to recognise what they are experiencing more easily.

People who experience anxiety are at an increased risk of experiencing panic attacks. However, having anxiety doesn't mean you will experience a panic attack.

Generally, episodes of anxiety last from a few minutes to about 30 minutes, although sometimes they can last even longer, and a sequence of these could be experienced over a few days. How long they last is likely to be determined by how frightened you might be of the symptoms you experience. Anxiety can go on for weeks, months or even years if it is not addressed.

How can you help yourself with the experience of panic attacks and anxiety?

There are a number of things you can do to help yourself when you are having a panic attack or feeling anxious. If you are in a public place and you are able to move to somewhere more private, it may be helpful. Some of these strategies can even be done in the most private place, the loo! It should be noted that many people have a natural resistance to practising these techniques – and self-care generally – but please believe that they do work.

SELF-REGULATION

Put simply, self-regulation is the ability to calm yourself down or self-soothe in response to having a strong reaction, like disappointment, panic, overwhelm, anxiety, fear, anger and grief, so that we can manage and control our emotions in a socially and personally acceptable way. The ability to care for yourself in this way supports you to identify when your feelings become aroused and how best to respond to stop such big feelings escalating further, enabling you to stay in control and make better or more informed choices in managing your emotions.

If you have had a panic attack or suffered from anxiety previously, you will recognise what is happening and it is helpful to accept what is taking place, even though it feels frightening. Remind yourself that you don't feel like this all the time, the sensations *will* pass, and you *will* be okay.

DO SMALL
THINGS WITH
GREAT
LOVE

SIGHING OUT: Take a deep breath in, but instead of just breathing out normally make a sighing sound as you breathe out. Sighing out like this pushes the breath out, enabling you to take a deeper breath in to fill the whole of your lungs and not just the top part of your lungs where we shallow breathe. It is especially helpful in releasing the immediate physical tension you may be holding when feeling overwhelmed or anxious. It is very helpful to practise this regularly.

BLOWING BUBBLES: You can buy a small bottle of bubbles to carry with you. A bit like 'sighing out' above, this can help regulate your breathing. By taking a deep breath in and then blowing as many bubbles as you can in one outbreath it can help regulate your breathing and calm you down. You don't have to concentrate on counting the breath, simply focus on taking a deep breath in and blowing out.

GROUNDING 1: Sit as far back in a chair as you can with your spine pressed against the back of the chair. This can feel very comforting, as if someone 'has your back' – enjoy that experience of connection and support.

GROUNDING 2: In a seated position, place both feet on the ground and push them down into the floor. As you do this, focus on your toes and the balls and heels of each foot connecting with the floor beneath you. Without judging, notice what it feels like and which parts of your feet actually meet the ground. Making connection with the ground beneath your feet can be very helpful when you feel a bit lightheaded and don't feel totally present.

GROUNDING 3: Lie on your back with your legs over the seat of a chair at a 90-degree angle. Focus on relaxing your back into the floor with your arms out to the side in a low V shape and stay there for about 15 minutes. As you breathe, notice your back making connection with the floor and your body becoming heavier and more relaxed. This is an effective technique to calm anxiety.

CONNECTING: Sitting back in your chair as in Grounding 1, place one hand on your chest, palm down. Move your hand around your chest until you sense that you have found the right place. You will have an immediate sense of where that place is when you have a strong feeling of comfort. Keep your hand there as you consciously breathe in and out. Placing your other hand over the top of the hand on your chest can offer you a stronger sense of connection and easing of tension.

CUDDLY TOY: Grab that cuddly toy you have had for years and just hug it to bits. If you don't have a cuddly toy, you could hold a pillow or cushion close to yourself. It might feel silly doing this but it can be comforting.

YOGA: Yoga is a very simple way of helping the body's nervous system to calm down and is a great way to self-regulate. There are classes available and many clips to follow on YouTube, ranging from a few minutes to an hour. Practising yoga for a few minutes will help lower your heart rate and relax your breathing and thus bring relief from anxiety and tension. However, doing yoga every day will help your body to get used to relaxing.

ORIENTING: Focus on different objects in the room. For example, everything that is red or blue, or listen to noises inside the room and outside of the room. Think about a small handful of things in your room that make you feel good and then collect them all together. Alternatively, you can look for five things you can see, four things you can touch, three things you can hear, two things you can smell, and one thing you can taste. You can use this technique effectively when you notice that you're starting to feel overwhelmed or anxious. It enables you to focus on using your senses to help you stay mindfully aware and in the present moment experience, and it supports you to regulate your feelings.

FIDGET TOYS: Grab a tangle toy, loom bands, beads, or any other small toy you can fidget with.

JOURNAL: Write down how you are feeling in the moment. Getting those thoughts that are running around your head down on paper can help a lot.

PLAYLISTS: Create a playlist of music you know will put you in a calmer mood. Music can have a direct impact on your energy levels, whether high or low. Equally, if you are feeling flat and numb, music that perks you up and makes you want to dance can be a big mood changer.

APPS: There are apps that can be helpful in the moments of anxiety. Take time to explore them; for instance, Stop, Breathe & Think; Calm; Happier; and Panic Relief.

If you have already experienced a panic attack or suffered from an episode of anxiety, below are suggestions to help improve how you feel generally so you are less likely to experience another panic attack:

Mood box: Create a mood box containing some of your favourite and most comforting things. You could include, for example, something that smells good, something that is tasty (e.g. your favourite sweets or biscuits), something with a texture that feels nice in your hands, and something bright and appealing to look at. You can dip into your mood box at any time, but it is especially helpful when you want to comfort yourself.

Exercise: Take regular exercise. Walking, running, swimming and boxing are just a few brilliant ways to manage stress and anxiety.

Food/diet: Try to eat no matter how anxious you might feel, especially when you don't have an appetite or feel a bit sick. Just eating something small can help with your energy and prevent you feeling even more low. At the very least, drink water to stay hydrated.

Rest: You can feel very tired after having a panic attack or suffering from an episode of anxiety and it is helpful to rest somewhere that feels safe and comfortable, ideally with someone you trust - even if you feel you want to be alone for a while.

Mindfulness: Everyone finds the practice of mindfulness difficult at first, but it can be a game changer in life. The trick is to notice what is happening in your body as well as what you are thinking about, without placing any judgement on yourself for experiencing the sensations or for having the thoughts that come up. Focusing mindfully on the present moment doesn't mean that feelings and embodied memories which are connected to the past stop coming up, but by staying mindfully present you can balance those feelings with the knowledge that you are not currently in that dangerous, frightening or alarming situation that you experienced in the past.

Breathing: We all breathe every minute of every day. The body knows what to do without you having to even think about it. However, it is helpful to practise a breathing exercise every day to support you at the times when you feel panicky and anxious and find yourself breathless, short of breath or holding your breath. When you start to feel your breath changing, breathe in deeply all the way down to your tummy to a count of four, hold your breath for a few seconds and then breathe out to a count of four and pause for a few seconds before breathing in again to a count of four. Repeat this pattern of breathing 10 times. You can practise this once, maybe first thing in the morning, or a few times each day and it will help to regulate your breathing and will support you when you feel the onset of a panic attack or anxiety.

Caffeine: Reduce your caffeine intake. It is a stimulant and can wind you up rather than relax you!

Alcohol and drugs: If you are already using alcohol and/or drugs you may have noticed that they can alter your mood in ways that don't always feel good. Alcohol and some drugs may appear to calm you down or get you energised, but before long they can also make you feel out of control, powerless, paranoid and even more panicky and anxious! Try to limit usage, particularly if you are having panic attacks or suffering from anxiety on a regular basis, to avoid feeling worse.

Talk: It can be very helpful to tell someone you trust that you're having panic attacks or suffering from anxiety. If you can describe what happens to you, that person might be able to notice those symptoms and help you in the future. It is also helpful to let them know how they can help you if/when this happens again.

Counselling: You might prefer to talk to someone who is completely independent and doesn't know your family and friends. A counsellor will work with you on your fears, difficult experiences and worries and support your emotional and mental health to recover.

HOW TO GET HELP

If you continue to feel overwhelmed it may be helpful to get some additional support. It's very important that you don't hold on to the experiences of overwhelm alone. They are a normal response to a traumatic, frightening or painful experience and are not a failing in you as a person. In getting help, others can support you to recognise this and validate your feelings. Talk to a trusted friend or family member, or to someone you feel you can trust such as a teacher, pastoral care or colleague, so that they can support you. Alternatively you can:

- Contact **Childline** for information, advice and support – **tel: 0800 1111** or online chat and email via **www.childline.org.uk**
- Find a local **counselling service** to help support you emotionally. A counselling professional can support you and help you process the feelings of overwhelm so they become more manageable. Your local doctor's surgery may be able to suggest a counsellor or you can look for a local service online, but ensure that the counsellors are registered with a professional body of practitioners such as:

  BACP – British Association for Counselling and Psychotherapy
  UKAHPP – UK Association of Humanistic Psychology Practitioners
  UKCP – UK Council for Psychotherapy
  BPS – British Psychological Society
  COSCA – Counselling and Psychological in Scotland
- See **'Places to Get Help'** (page 277) for a list of websites and helplines where you can get information and advice.

Chapter 11
DEVELOPING YOUR SELF-ESTEEM AND CONFIDENCE

Being with a partner who has hurt you, frightened you and treated you poorly and with disrespect can leave you feeling betrayed and broken. Although it can be difficult to believe you will ever rebuild your confidence to trust anyone ever again, you will. This chapter offers some ideas and strategies for supporting your self-esteem and building your confidence.

Self-esteem

Self-esteem is a combination of your level of confidence and self-worth, your qualities and abilities, and how much you respect yourself. When you are treated poorly over a period of time it can impact your level of self-esteem. Simply put, your 'estimation of self' means how you see yourself in comparison to others. If you believe you are 'good enough' then your self-esteem is in place and reasonably high. This means that you know you have self-worth and self-value and you are happy and content in yourself. However, if you don't think you are 'good enough' then you likely have a low self-esteem.

Your level of self-esteem affects the way you treat yourself and it shapes how you live your life. Having low self-esteem can be part of the reason you find yourself in difficult and uncomfortable relationships. When you feel this way it's not uncommon to want a partner to help you feel worthy, wanted and valued. It may lead you to believe that to feel good about yourself you need to be in a relationship whilst holding the unrealistic expectation that this will make you feel happier.

YOUR FIRST LOVE

SHOULD BE

YOURSELF

How To Build Your Self-esteem

Below are some things that you can do to build your self-esteem when you are feeling low:

Make a list or create a poster of all the realistic ways you can treat yourself or help yourself feel better and act on some of them, such as watching a film, having your favourite food and so on.

If you are isolating yourself from others, try to force yourself to be with the people who care about you. **Reach out** and talk to someone you can trust, such as a good friend or a relative. It helps to feel connected to others and can make you feel much better about yourself generally.

Take the time to **exercise**: when you move and are energetic your body releases hormones called endorphins, which make you feel better. Try running, taking brisk walks, cycling, swimming or any other form of exercise that increases your heart rate.

Practising **yoga** can help you to become more attuned to your breath and your body, and it can support the release of physical tension.

Alongside exercise is getting a good night's **sleep**: having proper rest enables the body to recover from stressful experiences. The combination of exercise and sleep will give you more energy to see everything more clearly and positively.

Think of something you have always wanted to do and **have a go**! It might be something you never thought you would be able to do, so the sense of achievement when you make it happen for yourself can be a big part of building your self-esteem.

Give yourself time to do **something creative** and try to do this without passing judgement. When creating something, it is important to work at your own pace. It can be a good idea to do some of these things with others, so you also benefit from their support.

Do something nice for someone else: help a friend, family member or neighbour do something they are struggling with – for example, offering to walk a neighbour's dog, baking a cake for your best friend or helping someone younger than you with their homework. **Helping someone else** can give you the 'feel-good factor': you will feel helpful, useful and even proud of yourself.

Remember that **feelings change**. The difficult feelings you might have now will come to an end because bad feelings do not last forever.

If you always do what you always did, you'll always get what you've always got.

Confidence

Confidence is something that everyone wants and most people think others have a secret formula to it. People talk about needing body confidence, confidence in their abilities, or being confident enough to stand up for themselves. You may think that to gain confidence you need good dress sense, an overly loud personality or amazing talent; however, **confidence is a mental attitude that you can cultivate**. Confidence is about feeling good in yourself rather than feeling good about how others see you.

Confidence is a belief in yourself – the quiet knowledge of being capable. It can include feeling happy or content with who you are and knowing that you are good enough for anything! People grow up with a greater or lesser degree of confidence and it is something you need to work at. It can take a very long time to feel truly secure in yourself and, despite appearances, even those who have confidence – even a lot of confidence – have days when they feel very unconfident in themselves.

You can also be confident in one aspect of yourself, for example your ability to play a particular sport or instrument, but feel very insecure about another aspect, like your body. We tend not to recognise that we are not born with confidence and that it is a skill: if you give it the amount of attention a footballer would give to practising a pass, or a gymnast gives to practising backflips on the barre, it will grow.

How To Develop your Confidence

You can adopt various strategies to help grow the pathways in your brain that emphasise confidence in yourself. They work when you make them a habit and part of your daily routine.

Change the way you hold yourself physically – stand and sit up straighter, lift your head and challenge yourself to look people in the eyes when you talk to them. Just as forcing yourself to smile can make you feel happier, standing confidently can make you feel more confident.

Don't dwell on your mistakes – literally everyone makes them. Pay attention to your mistakes and see what you can learn from them for the future. They are a natural way of learning how to navigate a situation and what not to do again.

Do something that makes you feel good about yourself. If you know you're good at something – whether it's music, running, doodling or mathematical equations – do some of that when you feel low to remind yourself that you have got a skill.

Ask yourself questions to **figure out who you are**: What do I love doing? What makes me happy? What am I afraid of? What would I like to change or stay the same about my life? What has changed in my life already? What is my dream for the future?

Surround yourself with people who lift you up. Having a partner or maybe friends who bring you down or make you feel 'less than' about yourself is not helpful, especially when you are trying to build your confidence. Ask yourself: How happy are you in your relationship? Who are my closest friends? How do my friends treat me? Whose company do I most enjoy? If you don't have a partner or any friends who act respectfully and positively towards you, seek them out!

Wear clothes that make you feel good but not invisible. Whether it be colourful dresses or t-shirts and jeans, wear the things that make you feel comfortable rather than what is most fashionable or what others might find acceptable. If it feels right, a further challenge would be to wear clothes that you would like to feel more comfortable in – such as a brighter t-shirt – or try arranging your hair differently and see how that makes you feel.

Confidence is **without a doubt** the best thing you can wear.

Listen to yourself. If your intuition tells you to wait an hour before answering that text, listen to it! If someone asks you to do something you don't want to do, say 'no'. If you don't want to answer immediately, take a breath to think or ask if you can come back to them later, because there's nothing wrong with going at your own pace.

Trust that your feelings are valid. There may be a reason you feel unconfident – for example, you made a mistake, you have low test scores, you're experiencing hormonal changes because of your period or are simply feeling super shy – but that doesn't mean your emotions aren't also happening. Acknowledge your feelings: you're allowed to feel things, and you're allowed to feel better.

Remember that **everyone else is human too.** (Yes, parents, carers and even teachers!) Everyone has good days and bad days. If you have a bad day, it doesn't reflect on you – you're not the reason someone else snapped at you and you're not the only reason you snap at yourself. Bear in mind that everyone is struggling with confidence and every person is trying to make sense of themselves and the world around them. Just take every minute, every hour and every day as it comes and communicate with others. If you let yourself off the hook and remember that others are moving through the world similarly to you, your confidence will grow.

Chapter 12:
STAYING SAFE ONLINE

Staying safe online is something you are taught throughout your school life. However, this knowledge can easily be forgotten when you are meeting people and developing relationships online. This chapter gives some pointers to help remind you of ways to ensure you stay as safe as possible online.

Experiences you may have had

If a partner or ex-partner has been abusing you in real life, they are likely to continue the same pattern of abuse online. They can use social media as a means to control and threaten you. If you are in or have been in a coercive relationship, you may have experienced one (or more) of the following:

- **Direct threats** – made to you, your family or someone you know online

- **Cyberbullying** – poking fun at you, humiliating and shaming you to as wide an audience as possible

- **Revenge porn** – threatening to expose sexual images of you online

- **Stalking** – constantly messaging you, presenting you with unwanted gifts, spying on you and turning up wherever you happen to be and making threats to you or your family

- **Creeping** – persistently checking up on you on social media by browsing your timeline, updates, conversations, photos/videos, profiles and friends; it can also include checking what you have written on other people's timelines or retweets. Creepers tend to hide the fact that they are creeping by not inviting, commenting or responding. It is not deemed 'harmful' and therefore is not an offence

- Being approached by **people using fake accounts** who say they are feeling lonely, vulnerable or upset as a lure to getting your full attention

- If you have shared your passwords with your partner/ex, your **personal accounts can be tarnished and monitored**, and they can send abusive messages to friends and family to isolate you

- Your partner/ex may also put spyware or GPS locators on your phone or computer and use these to **track your movements.**

Staying Safe

These are some basic tips for staying safe online that you should practise at all times:

- Don't post any personal information online that can identify you, where you live or the school or college you go to

- Don't befriend people you don't know

- Don't meet up with anyone face to face if you have only met them online

- Don't do anything sexual online

- Gran Alert – if you don't want gran to see it, don't post it

- If you see something online that makes you feel uncomfortable, unsafe or worried, turn it off and tell an adult

- Cover your webcam

- Your social media is an extension of you, not your whole self. If your followers don't know something about you, don't post it – only tell those who are truly your friends

- Everything you post online leaves a digital footprint. Try looking yourself up on Google to see what's out there and contact providers if you are unhappy with your findings and want something removed. Google algorithms change what different people see on the search page depending on their internet history, so you can use a 'Private Window' to get an authentic idea of your online presence.

Passwords

These are some basic things that you should always do where online passwords are concerned:

- Use a different password for each account
- Use multiple words – a sentence can work, for example 'I love dance music'
- Don't include personal information in your password
- Change passwords if you think someone knows them
- Make your passwords long
- Use a mix of characters
- Don't use memorable keyboard paths like 'qwerty'.

Social Media Safety

These are basic things you should always do when using social media:

- Use a strong password
- Password protect your device
- Don't share your password with partners or anyone else. Be selective with friend requests
- Go to privacy settings and turn on 'make account private' if the account allows it
- Turn off geographic location settings
- Go through the settings app on your phone to see what your apps have access to – camera, microphone, location – and turn off the ones you don't want or don't use frequently (you can always turn them back on), and switch location to 'off' or only when using a particular app

- On Instagram, turn off activity status so people can't monitor when you've been on. Hide your story from people, only allow @mentions and tags from friends to avoid seeing unwanted content, hide or block offensive comments
- Clear unwanted or unknown followers from time to time – don't be afraid to block them
- Log off when finished
- Never use social media to obtain emotional support
- Report abuse
- Use your report as evidence.

Remember that being on social media can make it much easier for you to be found. Social media posts are now widely cited as evidence in domestic abuse cases so keep records of the abuse you receive via your social media or on digital technology. **Do not reply to any abuse – log it as proof for when you need it.**

Using Apps To Get Help

Social media sometimes plays a role in the exit of an abusive relationship as it can be used as a means to contact others and escape. This may be the only way you can send a direct message and get help.

- Utilise private messaging on various apps so your messages can't be seen by your partner
- Disappearing videos and messages on apps like Snapchat are ways you can contact your family to ask for help

LOVE IS

SECURE

➤ If you are with your partner and feel unsafe or in danger you could turn on apps that identify your location so abuse services and family members can see where you are

➤ Use secret signals during video calls

➤ The Bright Sky app helps you find support services close to your current location

➤ The Hollie Guard app is activated by a shake of the phone and will alert your chosen contacts, pinpointing your location as well as recording audio and video evidence to their mobile phones.

HOW TO GET HELP

If you have met someone online and they are putting you under pressure to do things that make you feel uncomfortable, you can contact:

- **CEOP** for support if you are experiencing online abuse and are concerned about the way someone is communicating with you – **www.ceop.police.uk**

- **Childline** for information, advice and support – **tel: 0800 1111** or online chat and email via **www.childline.org.uk** If you are under 18 you can use the website to securely report nude/sexualised images to prevent them being uploaded: search for the 'Report Remove' tool and you will find clear instructions. When reporting in this way, it makes no difference whether you shared the image willingly or were coerced or groomed.

- See **'Places to Get Help'** (page 277) for a list of websites and helplines where you can get information and advice.

Chapter 13:
WHAT IF I WANT TO LEAVE?

Chapter 9 highlighted what behaviours to be alert for at the beginning of a relationship. As your relationship develops, you might recognise that you don't want to be with this particular partner for some or all of the reasons identified in the chapters on the Charmer, the Bully, the Mindmixer, the Taker and the Keeper. This chapter will guide you through the steps you can take to safely end the relationship and move on.

WHY MIGHT YOU FIND IT DIFFICULT TO LEAVE AN ABUSIVE RELATIONSHIP?

Viewed from the outside, many people assume it must be easy to leave an abusive relationship and ask: 'Why don't they leave?' For most people, being caught in an abusive relationship is outside of their experience so they can be forgiven for not understanding the complexities of the situation and that it is not simply a case of walking away. There is a long list of reasons, any of which could be experienced simultaneously (at the same time), making the thought of leaving too overwhelming to consider. It is how you can become trapped in an abusive relationship.

Some reasons why you might struggle to leave an abusive relationship are:

- you believe you are in love
- you are being 'love bombed'
- The 'kiss and make up' sex is worth it
- you think what's happening to you is normal
- you don't see what is happening as abuse
- you fear being alone
- you believe no one else will want you
- your partner promises they will change
- you believe you can change the way your partner behaves
- you believe your partner doesn't mean it
- your think your partner is a good dad or mum
- you are too emotionally invested
- you don't want to upset your partner
- you are worried your partner will hurt themselves
- you feel sorry for your partner

- you don't want to be blamed
- you fear the consequences
- your partner has made threats
- you are afraid of being harmed
- you are afraid of others being harmed
- you are afraid of being killed
- you physically can't leave
- your partner is blackmailing you
  (e.g. saying that they will share private information and images)
- you believe you deserve to be treated badly
- you have lost your confidence
- you are embarrassed
- you feel like a failure
- you feel like damaged goods
- you don't want to speak up because you think you won't
  be taken seriously
- you are scared of what your friends might say
- you go to the same school/college as your partner
- your partner is a family friend
- your partner is in the same friendship group
- you are afraid of losing status/popularity/friends
- your family likes your partner
- your friends like your partner
- It's against your cultural values to leave
- you don't want to be told 'I told you so'
- you don't want to face your parents
- you are pregnant
- your partner has given you an STI/STD
- you have become dependent on drugs supplied by your partner
- you are in debt
- you have no family or friends to turn to for support
- you have nowhere else to go/live
- you don't know how to leave.

Leaving an abusive relationship is never an easy thing to do whatever your age, but it can be done. If you are in an abusive relationship, you might be extremely reluctant to confide in adults who are older than you or authority figures. Maybe you fear that the concerns you have about your relationship will be ignored, minimised or ridiculed because adults, or people with more experience of relationships, have a tendency to underestimate the intensity of teenage relationships, thereby not taking them seriously.

This will have been made more difficult for you if, as a result of the Controller's influence on your life, you have damaged or lost your relationship with your parents or other significant adults who may be able to support you. In talking to an adult or authority figure you may also think you will lose your new-found independence and autonomy. You might fear being seen as immature or not mature enough to cope with making the right choices, and so you might prefer to confide in your friends or peer group.

If you are afraid of your partner, it can make things even more difficult. You may fear making the situation worse by talking to an authority figure. This is particularly worrying if the Controller attends the same school, college, youth club or workplace as you do. This would almost certainly increase any sense of fear you might have.

It may be that the culture or community in which you live wouldn't tolerate young people getting involved in dating or having intimate relationships, thereby making it more dangerous for you to seek help from someone within your community. Or perhaps you are already married and there is every expectation that you will stay married no matter how poorly you are being treated by your partner. In this case, even if you are desperate for help you would likely refuse to seek assistance from family or community members out of fear of reprisal, shame and bringing dishonour upon your family. Equally, seeking help outside of your community might also bring conflict within the family.

Issues of race could also influence your decision about whether to report an abusive partner. If you have been raised in a culture where racism or discrimination is present, it is understandable that you might be unwilling to discuss your abusive relationship with others outside your culture, racial community or family. Maybe you want to protect your partner because you share a common understanding, experience or cultural backdrop with them. These similarities can form an extra level of alignment with the Controller.

If you are pregnant, further challenges, complications and pressures need to be navigated. It is difficult being a single mum in today's society and it's even harder to be a teenage mum. You may find you are often blamed or harshly judged by the adults in your life, your peers and the wider society, as if it is 'all your fault'. But the belief that it is all your fault doesn't take into account the context of the coercive and controlling relationship you find yourself in and which may not be obvious to the person looking in from the outside.

Pregnancy may lead you to believe that you need to try and make it work with your abusive partner. You may hold the

idealised belief that they will change their behaviour because you are pregnant and you can be the happy family you dream of. Ironically, despite the abusive way your partner treats you, it is too easy to develop a sense of dependency on them because they are the 'father' of the baby. Sadly, studies have shown that during pregnancy abuse can increase significantly, by as much as 33 per cent. This puts you at a greater risk of experiencing further coercive and controlling behaviours. As a young pregnant woman, you may be less aware of your options. You can experience increased feelings of isolation, helplessness and self-blame, and all of this can be further used against you by the Controller.

Your sexual and gender identity may also influence your decision when it comes to speaking out about intimate relationship abuse. In addition to the normal confusion about gender roles and social norms, as an LGBTQ+ person you may face chastisement, severe criticism and put-downs. There may be no obvious or visible role models within your reach to seek help or support from. It may be that the relationship has been a secret and so you feel the need to keep working at it because there is nobody to turn to. Perhaps you haven't yet come out and the very real fear of being 'outed' prevents you from seeking help. Or maybe you did turn to your parents, but your relationship with them has deteriorated since they learned about your sexuality.

You **can still miss the relationship** even when you don't want it.

ENOUGH IS ENOUGH

Plates fall, the room has been smashed.
Not understanding how their mood has just crashed.
I hear the door slam and I tense up.
So quick I'm scared of what's going to happen next.
I grab my phone to try and make a text.
I hide my feelings so no one can see.
The true extent of their actions and what they're doing to me.
They smile, they laugh, they yell.
They say I'm ugly, trashy and that I smell.
I'm fed up with them making me feel so down and rough.
I'm leaving today, enough is enough.

How Will The Controller React?

Sadly, there is never an easy way to end a relationship because it inevitably makes at least one person feel bad, rejected or hurt. If you want to end your relationship with the Controller, they will work hard to prevent you from leaving. In their eyes, you are definitely not allowed to end the relationship; according to them, it can only end when they decide and not before. If you want things to be over, the Controller will feel as if they are losing control and will make every attempt to change your mind. They might try pursuing you constantly as a sign of how much they 'love' you, but this behaviour is only about enabling them to regain control. You can be sure that if they are ready to end the relationship, they would drop you like a lead balloon!

They will almost certainly turn on the charm offensive, perhaps because you 'fell for it' at the onset of the relationship. This return to the nice behaviours of the **Charmer** can feel very confusing because it instils **hope** at the very point you want to leave the painful **reality** of your relationship. They might apologise and make promises to behave differently. They might tell you more often that they love you and propose to you or ask you to get engaged. They might suggest you get serious and have a baby together, so you can be a family. They might shower you with gifts and compliments, show you more of the cheeky grin you love so much or take you out somewhere you have always wanted to go. Ultimately, you might start to believe that the person you first fell for at the beginning of the relationship is still there and that they really do care about you and want your relationship to continue.

What happens if these more loving gestures don't convince
you and you still want to end the relationship? The Controller
will step up their powers of persuasion with tactics like crying
or telling you a 'sob story' to demonstrate their vulnerability.
They might threaten or promise to hurt themselves by taking
an overdose or doing other forms of self-harm. Alarmingly,
they might even demonstrate this in front of you by grabbing
some tablets and threatening to take them there and then or
getting a knife and putting it to their wrist. They may even
go so far as to threaten to kill themselves. If you have been
coerced into feeling responsible for their wellbeing during
your relationship or guilty for abandoning them, you might be

tempted to give in at this point. The Controller coerces you to believe it would be your fault if they hurt themselves and living with the feeling of guilt would be too much to bear.

Despite how sympathetic you might feel towards your partner for how they feel or their difficulties, you may still be determined to end the relationship. Once the **Charmer** recognises that you aren't falling for any of their efforts to reel you back in and convince you to stay, they will change gear, resorting to the other behaviours of the Controller – those of the **Bully**, the **Mindmixer**, the **Taker** and the **Keeper**. If the Controller has made threats to hurt you in the past, you may believe that they will harm you or make life difficult for you if you try to leave.

The **Bully** will threaten to hurt you if you decide to leave or don't want to be in the relationship anymore. They might damage things that belong to you. They might intimidate you by walking past your house or standing on the other side of the street to let you know they are there. They may harass your friends and family. They might even threaten to kill you or family members or your pets.

The **Mindmixer** might threaten to tell other people your secrets and will definitely tell you that nobody else would go near you or want you.

The **Taker** might make threats to expose pictures of you on social media platforms.

The **Keeper** may constantly send messages, never let you do anything without them or say things about you on your social media. They may be digitally stalking you so they know where you are at any given time. They may tell you that you will never be free of them and that you will always have to look out for them. They may follow you everywhere, which can look — both to you and to others — as though they really want you and miss you; but in reality, these are all forms of stalking and harassment and are dangerous. Despite being very similar, stalking and harassment relate to different offences that can cause victims and those close to them emotional, psychological or physical harm.

HARASSMENT AND STALKING

The terms 'harassment' and 'stalking' are often used interchangeably to imply very similar behaviours and intention.

Harassment

Being harassed is when a person receives unwanted behaviour from someone that makes them feel distressed, humiliated or threatened. It includes:

- Sending unwanted communications by text, email, or letter, or via social media or visits
- Verbal or online abuse
- Physical gestures or facial expressions
- Images and graffiti.

The **Protection from Harassment Act 1997** (PHA) outlines harassment offences as 'causing alarm or distress' (section 2), and 'putting people in fear of violence' (section 4).

Stalking

Stalking is when a person experiences a repeated and persistent pattern of behaviour which is intrusive and causes them fear of violent or abusive behaviour, alarm and distress. It includes:

- **Sending unwanted communications by text, email, letter or visits**
- **Consistently sending unwanted gifts, e.g. flowers**
- **Following you or spying on you.**

The **Protection of Freedoms Act 2012** created two new offences, effectively identifying stalking as a criminal offence:

- **Section 2A:** Stalking – harassment which involves a course of conduct that amounts to stalking.
- **Section 4A:** Stalking, which can be committed in two ways, namely:
  - Stalking involving fear of violence; and
  - Stalking involving serious alarm or distress.

The law only requires two or more incidents for it to be identified as stalking.

Cyberstalking

Cyberstalkers have exactly the same intention as the harassers and stalkers who don't utilise digital technology. They will use social media, instant messaging and emails to cause you embarrassment and humiliation, and to threaten you. Their activities include:

- **Catfishing (luring someone into a relationship by adopting a fictional online persona)**
- **Virtually visiting you by using apps like Google Maps street view**
- **Hijacking your webcam**
- **Looking at geotags to identify your location.**

If you receive unwanted gifts and communications after you have made it clear that the relationship has ended, your ex-partner may talk to you as if you are still together – not accepting the relationship is over is a sign of danger! They might mention an upcoming anniversary in your relationship and how they had wanted to celebrate it with you – where they want to take you or what the future together could look like. However, this is all designed to tug at your heart strings and give you the much yearned-for hope that they can change and that they love you. This behaviour is about **control**.

Some of these behaviours may appear harmless when they are one-off gestures or incidents, but when put together, they form a pattern of behaviour. In many cases, stalkers believe that their behaviour is an appropriate and normal response to you ending the relationship.

If, having read this, you think you may have or are being stalked or harassed, you can do the following:

- <u>Say 'no'</u> to your ex-partner and tell them you don't want any further contact from them. Don't enter into a discussion about it (see 'No' box on page 142).

- <u>Keep a diary</u> of all the incidents, including location, time and who was present and exactly what happened. By precisely recording the incidents you will have a full picture of the harassment should you need to report your ex-partner.

- <u>Report</u> the harassment and stalking to the police, even if you only feel a little scared. Your ex-partner's behaviour could escalate at any time. Reporting could result in a prosecution if things continue.

- <u>Tell someone</u> what is happening. Encourage them to record anything they might see. They can also help you to stay safe by being with you.

- <u>Personal safety</u> is vital. Ensure your phone is charged so you can always call the police or a trusted family member or friend. Invest in a personal safety alarm with a built-in SOS button.

It is hard to understand how frightening stalking and harassment is until it happens to you. There is a myth that this behaviour is not dangerous until it involves violent behaviour. In fact, a lot of the stalking behaviour is about coercive control; it is mental and emotional abuse often dressed up as jealousy and possession. This does not make it any less dangerous. Coercive control, physical assault, threats to kill, stalking and harassment and sharing or exposing images of you online are all criminal offences, and should be taken very seriously.

When deciding that you don't want to be in the relationship any more because you aren't feeling happy or at ease with your partner and the so-called 'sob story' is no longer enough to hold you, the Controller's behaviour is likely to have a big influence on you. By making threats to hurt you or expose you in some way, you may have an increased sense of being powerless, fearful, vulnerable, isolated, helpless and potentially suicidal, believing that might be the only way out. With previous knowledge of your partner's abusive behaviours, you will fear the consequences of the Controller's threats and actions. You can feel defeated if you are trapped in a relationship you don't want to be in but are too scared to leave.

You may have a real sense of the danger you face; however, over the period of your relationship you might have become desensitised (i.e. so used to the negative experiences and feelings that you don't see them for real or feel them anymore). Even if you don't feel the full force of fear, it is important to recognise at this point that you are in a dangerous situation and need to seek help and support as safely as possible.

HOW TO GET HELP

Having read this chapter, you may recognise that you want to end your relationship. That would be a wise choice; however, it is not a decision to carry out alone. It can't be stressed enough how important it is to talk through ending an abusive relationship with someone supportive who you trust. It is the safest way forward because you are not best placed to always know exactly what level of danger you may face. This is not to suggest that you wouldn't be able to recognise danger when faced with it, but you may not be aware of how far the Controller is prepared to go to prevent you from leaving them. It is also possible that you haven't been in a situation like this before, so a trusted adult or professional can help to assess the danger you might be facing and enable you to access the right support. You can:

- Use **hand signalling** if you are online with a friend or family member but are unable to speak to them directly. Hold your hand up to the camera with your thumb tucked into your palm, and then fold your fingers down trapping your thumb in your fingers to indicate that you are trapped.
- Contact **Childline** for information, advice and support – **tel: 0800 1111** or online chat and email via **www.childline.org.uk** If you are under 18 you can report nude/sexualised images to prevent them being uploaded, whether you shared the image willingly or were coerced or groomed. On the website search for the 'Report Remove' tool and follow the instructions.
- Call **999** and talk to the police if you have been threatened and/or have concerns.
- Call **999** and then **55** if you need **police support but you are not safe to talk**.
- Use the **Hollie Guard** app, which is activated by a shake of the phone and will alert your chosen contacts, pinpointing your location as well as recording audio and video evidence to their mobile phones.
- Contact the **Suzy Lamplugh Trust** for information on stalking and staying safe from violence and aggression – **www.suzylamplugh.org**
- Call the **National Stalking Helpline 0808 802 0300** for advice.
- See **'Places to Get Help'** (page 277) for a list of websites and helplines where you can get information and advice. Many of the websites have chat facilities where you can talk to someone about leaving your relationship safely.

My Safety Plan

Below is the basis of your own personal safety plan to help you work out what you need to do to get out of an abusive relationship safely. It is not intended that you work through this safety plan alone. It is essential to ask for help because when you are in the middle of a particularly difficult situation and your emotions are running high, you can lose sight of the dangers you might face.

You may find it difficult to disclose to an adult older than you or authority figure what is happening to you in your relationship. Find someone to confide in who makes you feel reassured that you will be believed and not be judged, especially as you may feel a mixture of love, fear and dislike for your partner. Feeling love for someone even when they are hurting you can be very confusing. Remember that nobody chooses to find themselves in an abusive relationship. It takes huge courage to speak out and you deserve support at this difficult and worrying time.

Having the courage to speak out is the first hurdle in terms of taking control of the situation you face. The second hurdle is recognising that **you will need the support of others**. Ending an abusive relationship is not easy and can be a real challenge, and you will need support to work out the best way to manage the situation and how you can safely best help yourself.

The safety plan is written in the 'first' person using 'I' statements to enable you to speak with your own voice, considering your own individual needs and circumstances. By identifying and agreeing to what you think is possible, you are creating and 'owning' your safety plan. Written from your perspective, it should give real meaning and purpose to your plan.

Things I can do if I am with my partner and am not feeling safe because of them:

I could say or do the following to try and get away from my abuser safely.

Things I can do if I want to end the relationship:

- I will plan the break up and not do it suddenly
- I will break up by email or phone rather than risk doing it face to face
- I will only make the choice to do this face to face if I have a friend or trusted person with me
- I will be very clear that my decision is final.

The words I will use are:

The way they might react could be:

This is what I will tell people after I have ended the relationship:

Things I can do to keep myself safe at all times:

- ☎ Keep my phone charged and with me at all times
- 📞 Keep important numbers stored in 'Contacts'
- 💜 I can tell a family member or trusted friend what is happening in my relationship
- ✔ I will stay away from isolated places
- ✓ I will try to avoid places where my abuser or his/her friends hang out
- ☀ If I have to meet my abuser, I will take a friend with me and meet in a public place
- ✔ I will keep those I trust informed of where I am or what I am doing
- ✎ I can use a code word to alert friends or family if needed
- ✗ I will not answer my abuser's phone calls or texts
- ✖ I will not answer calls from unknown numbers
- ✂ I could block my abuser's number.

Things I can do to keep safe when socialising:

- ✖ I will not go out alone, but ensure I am with a friend(s)
- 📞 I will ask my friends to keep their mobiles with them so I can contact them if I get separated
- ✈ I will leave a situation I feel uncomfortable in
- ✌ I will spend time with friends who I feel safe with and supported by.

Things I can do to keep myself safe online:

- ✔ I will set all my online profiles to be as private and secure as possible
- 💜 I will only ever give my password to my parents or those I truly trust
- ➤ I will not communicate via social media

✗ I will not say or do anything online that I would not do in person

✎ I will save and record all abusive and threatening comments, posts or texts.

Things I can do to keep safe at school/college/work:

♥ I will ensure I am with a friend when walking to lessons

✓ I will have my lunch and spend breaks with friends or in an area where there are school/college staff or trusted colleagues nearby

✈ I will change my route to school/college/work if needed and ensure I travel with a friend

❝❝ I can talk to a trusted member of staff about what is happening to me

➡ I will talk to a member of staff about changing my timetable if needed.

Things I can do to care for myself when my abuser tries to make me feel bad about myself or when I remember the things they said and did that hurt me.

Things I can do that make me feel better:

_____

_____

_____

Things I can plan for the future are:

_____

_____

Conclusion

Congratulations on finishing the book! It is not easy tackling the subject of relationship abuse, especially when you are going through it: that takes courage.

Life is never straightforward, that is for sure. Many of the important lessons I have learnt about relationships have been the result of some of the worst things that happened to me in my early abusive relationships. That is how life works: you learn from your experiences. The fact that things have been bad doesn't mean everything will continue to be bad. It is my hope that the knowledge you have gained about the dynamics of abusive relationships and how to recognise these behaviours in your current and/or future relationships will enable you to make smarter and more informed choices from today onwards.

Here are some key takeaways for you to hold on to:

- You are not responsible for anyone else's behaviour. **The way you were treated was not your fault.**

- If you are in, or have been in, an abusive relationship, the way you feel about yourself is a direct result of how you were treated by the Controller. **There is nothing wrong with who you are as a person.**

- **Feelings change.** How you feel about someone or something now, today, will ease over time. The pain of leaving an abusive relationship can feel huge and overwhelming, but the hurt will subside, and you can move on. You can and will go on to meet lovely partners who will treat you with respect, love and care.

- **You are brave, strong and gutsy.** Hold on to these strengths and build on the self-belief that you are lovely just as you are.

❤

I wish you every success in the choices you make.

I CELEBRATE MY QUALITIES & STRENGTHS

MY PERSONAL RIGHTS

I HAVE THE RIGHT TO PRIVACY AND MY OWN PERSONAL SPACE.

I HAVE THE RIGHT TO SPEAK OUT AND EXPRESS MY IDEAS AND OPINIONS.

I have the right to be respected for my beliefs and opinions even if they differ from those of my peers.

I have the right to study, learn and aspire.

I have the right to make mistakes without being ridiculed.

I HAVE THE RIGHT TO CHANGE MY MIND AT ANY TIME.

I HAVE THE RIGHT TO SAY 'NO'.

I have the right to own my body, thoughts, opinions and property.

I have the right to live without fear and confusion from my partner's anger.

I have a right to leave a relationship.

I HAVE THE RIGHT TO PRIVACY.

I HAVE THE RIGHT TO BE TREATED WITH LOVE, CARE AND RESPECT AND AS AN EQUAL.

I have the right to choose and spend time with friends and family.

Adapted from the Washington Attorney General's Teen Dating Violence Guide.

GLOSSARY

Abuse – Treating something or someone badly by being verbally or physically cruel, i.e. inflicting harm.

ADD – Attention Deficit Disorder

ADHD – Attention Deficit Hyperactive Disorder

Aspire – To hold particular goals, dreams or ambitions for your future.

Assumptions – Something you assume or take for granted.

Coercion – Control by force; making you do something you do not want to.

Consent – Giving permission for something to happen or agreeing to do something and being comfortable with that decision.

CPS – Crown Prosecution Service

Cyberbullying – A form of bullying when someone is repeatedly made fun of online through any form of digital technology – by emails, messaging and postings on social media.

Cyberstalkers – People who threaten or intentionally embarrass their victims using technology. They have the same intention as non-digital stalkers but rely on technology such as social media, instant messaging and emails to do this. Everything on the internet can be used by cyberstalkers to make unwanted contact with their victims.

Deadnaming – Purposefully referring to a person who is gender-fluid or transgender by their birth name rather than their chosen name.

Desensitisation – A state where you have become so used to negative experiences and feelings that you don't see them for real or feel them anymore.

Dissociation – A disconnection from your thoughts, feelings, memories and surroundings. It is an entirely normal response to overwhelming trauma.

Domestic violence and **domestic abuse** – Both terms mean the same thing and include physical and non-physical forms of abuse.

Expectations – Sense of something expected happening or thinking and presuming it ought to happen.

Flashbacks – A re-occurring memory of a past trauma, where you feel like you are re-living the traumatic event as if it is happening again.

Gender – The state of being male, or female or other in relation to the social and cultural roles that are considered appropriate for men and women.

Grooming – When someone builds a relationship, trust and emotional connection with a child or young person so they can manipulate, exploit and abuse them.

Harassment – Unwanted behaviour from someone else that makes you feel distressed, humiliated or threatened. Examples of harassment include: unwanted phone calls, texts, letters, emails or visits, abuse (verbal or online), physical gestures or facial expressions or images and graffiti.

Harassment injunction – Can be applied for against any person who has harassed or stalked you, or put you in fear of violence by deliberately causing you distress on two or more occasions. For example, the defendant (i.e. your abuser) is forbidden from coming within 200 metres of the home of the claimant (you).

Harassment warning – The police listen to the description of your abuser's behaviour but decide not to take any further legal action at that time. As an alternative they can issue the abuser with an informal harassment warning. These are also known as harassment warning notices or police information notices (PINs).

HBV – 'Honour-based violence' is the term used to describe violence committed within the context of the extended family that is motivated by a perceived need to restore standing within the community, which is presumed to have been lost through the actions or behaviour of the victim.

Homophobic A dislike or prejudice against people in gay relationships or who identify as LGBTQ+.

Hyper-vigilant – The experience of being constantly tense and 'on guard'. It can occur in an environment where you perceive an extreme threat or danger and your brain goes into high alert.

Hypo-vigilant – Experiencing yourself as numb, disconnected, flat or shut down as a result of traumatic experience(s).

IDVA – Independent Domestic Violence Adviser

Injunction – An injunction can be applied for through a County Court to forbid an abusive partner doing certain things such as contacting you directly or indirectly, going to your home address, place of work, college or school.

Intimidation – The use of threats to persuade or frighten you, as with the Bully.

ISVA – Independent Sexual Violence Adviser

LGBTQ+ – Lesbian, gay, bisexual, trans, queer/questioning with the plus sign signifying gender identities and sexual orientations that are not specifically covered by 'LGBT'.

Overwhelm – The experience and effect of strong emotional feelings.

Peer – Person of equal standing with another (you and your friends or year group).

Perpetrator – Someone who has committed a crime or a violent or harmful act.

Persuasion – Convincing and coaxing you to do or believe something.

Restraining order – May be issued to protect you if the abuser is charged by the police and the case goes to the criminal courts. A restraining order can be made even if the abuser is not found guilty. Breaking a restraining order is a criminal offence.

SARC – Sexual Assault Referral Centre

Social worker – A person who works for social services or for a private organisation providing help and support for people who need it.

Soyboy – A derogatory way to describe guys who are not typically masculine.

Stalking – A pattern of fixated and obsessive behaviour which is repeated, persistent, intrusive and causes fear of violence or causes alarm and distress in the victim.

Threats – Making clear the intent to punish or cause harm if you don't do as you're told.

Victim – A person who has been hurt, abused or killed or has suffered as a result of the actions of someone or something else.

YDVA – Young Person's Domestic Violence Adviser

Places to Get Help

Below is a list of useful websites and helplines most of which are free to access:

www.respectnotfear.co.uk is an informative, interactive and user-friendly site for young people to learn about teenage relationship abuse, how to identify it and how to get help. It was created by the Nottinghamshire Domestic Violence Forum.

www.thehideout.org.uk is the Women's Aid website for young people. It was created to help children and young people understand domestic abuse, and how to take positive action if it's happening to you.

National Domestic Violence Helpline 0808 2000 247 (24 hours) can be called if domestic violence is happening at home. The service is usually for people over the age of 18 but help may be available if you are 16 years old or over.

www.refuge.org.uk offers help and advice to women and young girls in abusive relationships.

www.disrespectnobody.co.uk is a Home Office website to give young people information about respectful relationships in all contexts, including relationship abuse, consent, rape and sexual harassment.

thisisabuse.direct.gov.uk is a Home Office website to give young people information about domestic abuse and teenage relationship rape.

www.childline.org.uk offers games, advice and help for young people on a range of issues. **Helpline 0800 1111** can be called to speak to someone about any relationship difficulties you or someone you know is having with their partner. If you are under 18 you can report nude/sexualised images to prevent them being uploaded, whether you shared the image willingly or were coerced or groomed. On the website search for the 'Report Remove' tool and follow the instructions.

www.thestudentroom.co.uk The Student Room is currently the UK's largest student community. The 'Relationships and Health' section gathers together the best relationship and health articles and latest discussions from the health and relationships forums.

loveisrespect.org provides key information to young people and has good interactive resources, and is extremely easy to navigate. Although it is an American website almost all the content is valid and applicable to the UK audience.

www.womensaid.org.uk is a national organisation working to provide life-saving domestic abuse services for women and children including refuge and support. Visit the 'Information and Support' section for ways to get in touch.

www.loverespect.co.uk Provides advice about relationships and abuse for young people.

www.mensadviceline.org.uk Mens Advice Line 0808 801 0327 is a confidential helpline for men experiencing domestic violence from a partner or ex-partner (or from other family members). This number is good to use whether you are in a same-sex or heterosexual relationship.

www.mankind.org.uk ManKind Initiative Helpline 01823 334244 offers support for male victims of domestic abuse and domestic violence.

www.safeline.org.uk National Male Confidential Helpline 0808 800 5005 provides a specific service for males but also offers specialist emotional support, information and advice to *anyone* affected by sexual abuse or rape in England and Wales.

www.survivorsuk.org offers an inclusive service welcoming anyone who identifies as male, trans, non-binary, has identified as male in the past, or anyone who feels that they are the right fit for them. **tel: 02035 983898**

www.galop.org.uk Helpline 0800 999 5428 offers support to lesbian, gay, bisexual and transgender people experiencing biphobia, homophobia, transphobia, sexual violence or domestic abuse.

www.brokenrainbow.org.uk Helpline LGBT Domestic Violence 0300 999 5428 (free)

www.gov.wales/livefearfree Live Fear Free Helpline 0808 8010 800 (free) provides a Welsh/English bilingual information service that helps and guides people who are victims of abuse, and are in need of information or access to support services in Wales.

www.karminanirvana.org.uk UK Helpline 0800 5999 247 offers support to victims of honour-based abuse and forced marriage.

www.southallblacksisters.org.uk is for women, children or young people who are Asian, African-Caribbean or other minority group, who are experiencing domestic or sexual violence (including forced marriage, dowry abuse and honour crimes).
tel: 0208 571 0800 provides information, advice, advocacy, practical help, counselling and support in English, Hindi, Punjabi, Gujarati and Urdu (interpreters are used for other languages).

www.ikwro.org.uk IKWRO supports females from Middle Eastern, North African or Afghan communities and can help you if you are at risk of honour-based violence, forced marriage, female genital mutilation and/or violence. It provides confidential advice, advocacy, and individual and group counselling. **tel: 0207 920 6460** offers services provided in Farsi, Arabic, Kurdish, Dari, Pashto, Turkish and English.

www.lifecentre.uk.com Lifecentre services are for women and men, girls and boys of all ages and backgrounds. **tel: 0808 802 0808** and **text: 07717 989022** both offer support for young people who have had or are experiencing sexual abuse or unwanted sexual contact.

www.rapecrisis.org.uk offers advice about rape and sexual violence and has the contact details for your nearest Rape Crisis Centre and Sexual Assault Referral Centre (SARC).

www.bishuk.com is 'a guide to sex, love and you' for young people (all genders/ sexualities) over the age of 14 who are (or are thinking about) having sex and relationships.

www.brook.org.uk is a service (including webchat) about anything related to sexual health. **Under 25's phone or text chat 07537 402024** offers support and signposting anywhere in the UK.

www.kooth.com is an online mental wellbeing community for under 18 year-olds that offers free, safe and anonymous support via live chat, an online magazine and discussion boards.

www.ceop.police.uk **tel: 999** in an emergency. Child Exploitation and Online Protection (CEOP) is a law enforcement agency to keep children and young people safe from sexual exploitation and abuse.

www.thinkuknow.co.uk provides the latest information on the sites to visit, mobiles and new technology. You can find out what's good, what's not good and what you can do about it. There is a place on the website to report if you feel uncomfortable or worried about someone you are chatting to online.

www.swgfl.org.uk/Staying-Safe/So-you-got-naked-online So You Got Naked Online offers help and advice for young people who put a sexting image or video online and have lost control over that content and who it's being shared with. Produced by the South West Grid for Learning.

www.thatsnotcool.com is an American website focusing specifically on digital and social networking abuse with activities and animation. It is very accessible and user friendly for young people.

Escape The Trap

He pushed me, he hit me, he slapped me and then
I thought it was over, but it started again.
He told me he loved me, I start to ask why,
Is part of loving someone to make them cry?

I really do love him and want this to work,
What can I change for him to stop causing hurt?
I say I'll forgive him, and take him back,
It started again with just a light slap.

My friends think I'm lucky to go out with him,
His mates think he's cool and look up to him.
I want to tell someone but where do I turn?
I feel so embarrassed, should I just learn

That this is expected from boys in my school
I feel kind of silly, I feel such a fool.
I thought relationships were different, I thought they were kind,
My Mum's didn't work out, is it all in my mind?

That love should be special and not cause such pain,
My head is in turmoil then it all starts again.
He pinched me, he shoved me, he made fun of me.
Not just in private but for all to see.

I feel so humiliated, I feel so ashamed,
So, I do as he says so his love can be gained.
He hugs me; he kisses me for all to see,
He pushes his body right up to me.

He fumbles; he strokes me, and whispers it's me
I feel his hard cock push right up to me.
He says he can't wait, he grabs my hand,
He rubs his hard cock with the palm of my hand!

He says he wants more as my friends look on,
I feel I must please him, so he carries on
I have no voice to say please, please won't you just stop
He just carries on, right on the spot.

I feel so relieved it's over at last,
Everyone's gone, I'm alone at last.
I lay there in silence, tears run down my face,
My knickers are torn, well at least the lace.

I feel really sore; I guess you just do,
The others had done it, so I needed to too.
I stand up and walk which is so hard to do,
I want to run home but what to?

I go to the toilet to wash away tears,
When I enter the classroom, everyone stares.

This was my first time, it happened so fast
I thought it would be special; it's just not a blast.
I want to escape this; I want my life back,
I see a small poster saying, 'Escape the Trap'.

What is this? Is this for me?
I go along anyway just to see.
I'm so surprised there are others like me
Who'd just gone alone as they wanted to see?
What was on offer to help you amend?
I don't need a bully. I just need a friend.

The poems included in this book have all been written by young people who have completed the Escape the Trap programme with Lighthouse Women's Aid, Suffolk; Young Women's Housing Project, Sheffield; and others offered with express permission but not to be acknowledged.

ESCAPE THE TRAP

ACKNOWLEDGEMENTS

I would like to thank those who offered me endless support in the process of writing *When Love Bites*: Paula Devaux, Roz Davidson, Esther Egerton, Cheryl Ansell, Deidre Duffy and my daughter Evie Press. This experience was made so much easier because of your encouragement. There are others who have supported me with their patience. Working full-time and writing in my spare time has meant that I have had less time to spend with much treasured friends and family.

My heartfelt thanks go to my husband Paul who has tirelessly kept me replenished with care and warm hugs whilst writing.

I would also like to thank those who worked alongside me to support the production of *When Love Bites*: Barbara Cheney for her meticulous attention to detail throughout the editing process; Nic Davies for superb design of the book and endless support; Etta Saunders Bingham for her astute insights and encouragement; and lastly – but not least – Dave Shephard for creating the wonderful tattoo images that illustrate the themes in the book.

Deepest appreciation and thanks to my mother, Marion Press, for persistently demonstrating the importance of standing up for those without a voice, doing the right thing even when it feels difficult, and knowing the privilege of helping someone along their personal journey.

Lastly, my sincere thanks to the thousands of survivors of relationship abuse with whom I have worked. I thank you for everything you have shared with me and taught me. I have carried your stories with me over three decades and I hope that I have given them a voice in supporting those who read this book.

AFTERWORD

At some point in your life, you may see an opportunity to use your experiences of abuse to help others. It may be tomorrow, next week, next year, or when you are much older. It won't necessarily be an easy thing to do, and you should only step in and offer support when you feel ready and secure in yourself. There is no obligation to step forward but be aware that one of the most powerful things you can do with your experiences of abuse is to use them to help someone else. For some people the opportunity simply doesn't arise; for others, their instinct tells them not to get involved – and this inner voice should be respected.

Some ways of helping are:

- Support a friend in a similar situation by validating their experience and feelings and pointing them in the direction of appropriate advice, support and counselling.

- If you are old enough, consider volunteering for a local domestic abuse service or community group that is raising awareness about intimate relationship abuse, coercive control, sexual coercion and/or healthy relationships. The opportunity to inform and share your knowledge with others – even with just one person – may mean that they avoid getting further trapped in their abusive relationship and are more able to make new and informed choices. It will empower you, too, to know you have put your insight, knowledge and experiences to good use.

- Join a march or peaceful protest that raises awareness around such issues as relationship abuse; supporting the victim through the justice system; misogyny as a hate crime (hostility based on sex or gender); educating school, college and university communities; freedom and liberty to walk the street without fear of danger, etc.

Most importantly, and when you feel able, carry on the conversation. Your testimony and experience are meaningful and keeping the conversation going about all the issues discussed in this book is so important. Intimate partner abuse is of pandemic proportion. It happens in every community across the world and it is up to everyone to talk about it so that it no longer remains the shameful and isolating experience that it has always been. Young people deserve the much-needed support to understand their experiences, and to recover and grow into future healthy, adult relationships.

ESCAPE THE TRAP

Escape the Trap is an innovative programme that was created in acknowledgement of the rising number of young people who are vulnerable to teenage relationship abuse. This learning resource was **developed alongside young people** and is delivered using a variety of activities and exercises to engage and develop discussion and encourage reflection.

Over eight weeks, the programme supports young people to **uncover the reality of teenage relationship abuse**. Young people in any relationship (including LGBTQ+) which they perceive to be intimate need the opportunity to explore and identify:

- their expectations of relationships;
- the grooming process that is often associated with sexual exploitation;
- patterns of behaviour which seek to coerce and control them, particularly sexual coercion;
- the use of digital technology and social media as a mechanism for control; and
- warning signs of controlling behaviour within the relationship.

Understanding how such behaviour impacts the way young people feel about themselves enables them to navigate their way to making healthier relationship choices which support their mental health and wellbeing. The programme also encourages young people to **explore how being treated with respect, care and love might be experienced**.